Spirit Relations:

Your User-Friendly Guide to the Spirit
World, Mediumship and Energy

Spirit Relations:

Your User-Friendly Guide to the Spirit World, Mediumship and Energy

Bill Duvendack

Megalithica Books

Stafford England

Spirit Relations: Your User Friendly Guide to the Spirit World, Mediumship and Energy by Bill Duvendack
© 2017 First edition

The rights of Bill Duvendack to be identified as the author of this work have been asserted by him in accordance with the Copyright, Designs and Patents Act, 1988.

Editor: Jennifer Garlich
Layout: Taylor Ellwood
Cover Design: Isis Sousa

ISBN: 978-0-9955117-5-0
MB0189

Set in Island Roman and Book Antiqua

A Megalithica Books Publication
An imprint of Immanion Press
info@immanion-press.com
http://www.immanion-press.com

Table of Contents

Dedication

This book is dedicated to my haters and those that intentionally avoid supporting me. Thank you for the fuel for this work.

Introduction

Why did I use such a direct and abrasive dedication, you ask yourself? Everything in existence is energy. As the law of conservation of energy in physics states, "energy can be neither created nor destroyed, but rather it transforms from one state of being into another." Hence, no matter what energy is sent my way, I'll use it as I see fit, transmuting it in the process as per the ancient practice of alchemy. Thus at the end of the day it can easily be said that to communicate with spirits and the spirit world, one should think in terms of energy. Yes, this statement is something very similar to what Nikola Tesla said, and it holds just as true today as it did when he stated it. Non-physical entities are easier to work with if you keep this in mind during your work.

However, there is another point to be aware of when dealing with the spirit world and spirit entities, and that is that everything has a vibration. Things range from a slow vibration, like a block of concrete, to a high vibration, such as light. Nothing is truly solid in existence, and thus we have a sliding scale to use. When interacting with the spirit world, it is wise to keep this in mind, as not all the entities you meet in there are of the same type and vibration, but all are energy at their essences, just as we are. Thus we can interact with lower vibrational beings as much as we work with higher vibrational beings.

If you keep these two points in mind when dealing with spirits and the spirit world, you can have more success in a safer way than a lot of people that may not stop to remember these points. Keeping these in mind also helps to frame what we discuss in the following pages. Thus when I use terms like "energy" and "vibration," you now have a frame of reference.

More on both of these points will be revealed in this text, but for now I simply mention these for clarification.

Recapping things then, it can be seen that interacting with the spirit world is a mix of vibration and energy. Thus there is no moral imperative. It is a skill, just like anything else. While not everyone may manifest skills to the same strength, this is just as true regarding any skill. I have known some of the most immoral spirit workers, but have also met some of the brightest ones, too.

Let us enter into the world of spirit where we will find many wondrous sites, but we will also find that all things in reality are a sliding scale of grey. Mutual exclusivity, synchronicities, Occam's razor, and other critical thinking skills are very helpful to use when we undertake this journey. After all, being a spiritual person simply means that you are one that works with the spirit world, and has no moral or ethical implications. After all, it is wise to keep in mind that we are all energetic spirits having a physical incarnation.

Bill Duvendack
Summer Solstice 2016

Part One: The Energetic Person

I begin this book by focusing on the energetic body of an individual rather than just jumping into spirit contact because as I said in the introduction, everything is energy and vibration. Thus before we address communicating and working with spirits, it would be wise to clarify our own energetic structure. Not only does this create context; it also fulfills the Hermetic axiom of "as above, so below, as within, so without." By becoming aware of our energetic body and learning techniques to work with it, we further empower ourselves to become fit receptacles for spirits and spirit work. Anyway, let's get back to the topic: the Etheric Double.

Chapter 1: The Etheric Double

The etheric double is a term that comes to us from Theosophy, and it is the term I prefer to use because of its clarity. The etheric double is a term that is used to represent the energetic body of an individual. Yes, there are different terms from different cultures that could just as easily be used, ranging from the fetch in the Celtic tradition to the different pieces of the soul from ancient Egypt. However, the problem with those terms is that they are not clear. For example, if you're not familiar with the Celtic tradition, then the term "fetch" is a game you play with a dog. If you work with a belief system that uses exclusionary terms like this, then by all means feel free to use them instead of "etheric double," but in this work I'll be sticking with "etheric double," so you may have to adjust a few times. The underlying principles I will be writing about cross cultures though, so the translation should be easy to make.

In short, the etheric double signifies the energetic side of the human being. Spiritualism has addressed this in their belief that man (generic term for human rather than a gender concept) in the physical world and man in the energetic world can communicate and work together. This has been measured to a certain degree of accuracy in the beginning of the 20th century with the experiments of Dr. Duncan MacDougall[1]. He and fellow doctors performed measurements on people that were near death, and even after accounting for air leaving the lungs, bodily fluids being discharged and other variables, there was still a loss of 21 grams that couldn't be explained. Thus the theory is that the soul weighs 21 grams. True, this is still a theory to this day, and further research would be needed, especially since we have more accurate testing devices now, but the fact of the matter remains that there is a loss that occurs at the moment of death, and this could be considered the weight of the soul. When animals died during his research, there was no perceived loss of weight, yet I believe all of us are confident in the fact that animals have souls. This is one of the weaknesses of his theory, but is also an opportunity for further exploration.

The etheric double is more than just the aura, as it encompasses much, much more, as we will discuss in the first section of this book. The aura is only part of it, but it is the one that is the most commonly known to most readers and seekers. The chakras are part of the etheric double, as is the energetic heart field. I will go into more detail about this later, so bear with me a moment. One of the things I learned through geometry many years ago is that if something is true, so is its converse, and when I learned more about metaphysics, this became profoundly truer due to the fact that we live in a polarity based reality. Thus it completely makes sense that there is an energetic counterpart to our physical form. This is also reinforced by the fact that, as we've learned from astrophysicists, matter and what we see is only approximately ten percent of all reality, with dark matter making up more of the multiverse than visible matter. Our body produces an energetic double and energetic field that can only *somewhat* be quantitatively studied due to the limits of scientific tools. Hence to me, the idea of an aura and of energetics like the type we're discussing are scientific truisms rather than subjective beliefs. Yes, religion and spirituality embraced this idea long ago, but up until approximately the last one hundred years, this was something that was relegated to beliefs, and now it has become perceived scientific reality. Can more research be done in this area?

---

[1] http://www.historicmysteries.com/the-21-gram-soul-theory/

Emphatically yes, and I encourage critical thinking when exploring this subject! However, the groundwork has been laid that this is simple science, and validates aeons of religious beliefs. Yes, the 21 grams theory is just a theory at this point, but to be fair, gravity is still just a theory too, so that detail becomes highly irrelevant, but worth keeping in mind nonetheless. Our scientific instruments are still developing, becoming more finely tuned as we grow and mature, and things that were fantasy as recently as fifteen years ago have now been proven to be truer than believed. An excellent example of this can be found in the telepathy experiments conducted in the early part of the 21st century by Harvard University researchers[2]. While more study is obviously needed, subtle energy phenomena like this are being studied and explored now more than ever, and while no concrete hard science results exist, it is obvious that we are on the right path with the research and technology that is currently available to us. Concepts that have been relegated to beliefs are now being brought into the scientific community, thus merging spirituality and science. However, this merging is a concept to be discussed at a later time. It is simply enough for now to know that this exists, and that each day may bring a glaring revelation that solves so many riddles of yore.

Simply put, while there are a lot of beliefs out there that have to do with the aura and the energetic body of a person, there is a growing amount of evidence that is telling us this is not just a belief, but rather scientific concepts that simply haven't been able to be measured clearly and via scientific methodology in recent history. It is only now that we are coming into greater clarity about who we are as a species. With this comes greater empowerment and an increased understanding of who we are and what we're capable of.

The Chakras

It is best to start off with addressing the mechanisms that trigger these energy fields rather than the fields themselves, so we will

---

[2] http://www.smithsonianmag.com/innovation/scientists-prove-that-telepathic-communication-is-within-reach-180952868/?no-ist

discuss the chakras and the chakra system. The term "chakra" is a Sanskrit word, and as is true with many Sanskrit words, there is no specific English word that it translates to. The closest meaning that you get is either "wheel," or "spinning." For all practical purposes, both of these meanings are true, for the chakras can be both seen as wheels, and also spinning at the same time. The language stretches back thousands of years, and thus is one of the oldest languages in existence. This is not the time or the place to enter into a dissertation of the history of Sanskrit, but rather we will continue with our discussion of chakras and the chakra system.

Going beyond popular information, I would like to address the chakra system in a slightly different way than a lot of other authors do. This is one of the main reasons for writing this book. Some people perpetuate false or inaccurate information because they received it from a trusted source, and thus take it verbatim. In this information age, critical thinking skills are more necessary than previously, and thus they are almost required in order to sift through the dross. Unless we check our information, we are taking it on faith, which is a dangerous thing to do when it comes to energy manipulation, whether having to do with our own energetic form or beings that are pure energy and spirit. Keeping critical thinking in mind during the reading of this text also lays the ground work for a concept I will address in part two, which is the concept of testing your spirits. This is a procedure that is very important when dealing with spirits, but with repetition it becomes easier to do.

Now let us take a closer look at the chakras (pronounced ch-ah-kras, with a hard 'ch', like in the word 'chalk'). In short, they are interdimensional energy vortices that exist in the etheric double. For the most part they run down the central body of a person, and exist from the bottom of the feet up to and above the head. While they don't exist physically, their states of being can impact life on a physical level. For example, if someone has heart problems on a physical level, this is usually seen as a manifestation of etheric heart center issues. The common metaphysical teaching behind this is that when there is something wrong in the energy body, it trickles down to the physical form. However, to a certain extent, the opposite is also very true. If someone gets injured near one of these chakra locations, it can damage the energetic form as well. While this is the lesser of the two scenarios, this is worth keeping in mind nonetheless because it shows a serendipity and synchronicity, which shows an elegance of the human form on all planes. These chakras exist throughout all of the bodies a person has. These energy vortices swirl around and spin, much like a wheel does, and they can be manipulated to produce great changes and effects in the body and the life of the individual. This premise is the basis for the Hindu discipline of mantras. Sanskrit and Hinduism are so intertwined that you can't really study one without studying the other. Mantras come from Hinduism, and in short they are a form of spiritual technology that morphs the energetic body of an individual in a particular fashion to produce desired results. As the energy field of an individual changes, so too do the experiences and realities an individual experiences. What an individual emits from an energetic level can be changed and altered through discipline, intent, and mantras to change the experiences of life. This can address everything from bringing in love and prosperity to changing situations that we go through in life. Hence we are not just talking about mental situations here, but also physical world situations.

In detail, it is worth noting at this point that the term mantra is a Sanskrit word that means an utterance or string of utterances that one speaks that can have spiritual or psychological influences. Here again it is worth keeping in mind that there is no clear cut English translation of the word, so you may find that definitions vary slightly from translator to translator. I mention this here because a common flawed teaching is that any sacred phrase is a mantra, but that is not true. The only mantras that exist are the ones that come from Hinduism. Therefore, words or phrases that could be seen as parallel mantras in other belief systems are really not mantras since they're not based in Sanskrit, but conceptually they are the same, and thus the term has been hijacked in modern times to include belief systems other than Hinduism, and other words and phrases of power as well.

To continue, we should be aware that Sanskrit and Hinduism are two very old traditions, and because of this, variances have come up over the years. This is important to know because there are a few different beliefs when it comes to chakras. One tradition says that there are "X" number of chakras, while another tradition says that there are "Y" number of chakras. Do your research and decide for yourself what scheme you will use, because no one tradition that I know of is wrong, nor is there a tradition that is right, but rather these are variances on a theme, and in this case the theme is the chakra system. For the most part, most traditions agree that there are at least three chakras, so this is a safe starting point. The placement of these are in the lower abdomen, the heart, and at the crown of the head or slightly above the head. The popular concept of working with seven chakras is believed to come from the writings of Arthur Avalon at the beginning of the twentieth century and his book called *The Serpent Power*, which is a translation of an older text named the *Satcakranirupana*, believed to have been written approximately 1577 AD[3]. It is easy to see how the timeliness of his translation had a major impact, but as the world has become more integrated, more information has been made available to the serious student, and thus another layer of mysteries has been removed. No, the concept of the chakras does not begin around 1577, but rather they are written about as far back as the eighth century BCE. The treatise that Avalon translated was simply a retelling in a lot of ways, and it specifically deals with the chakras and kundalini, which we'll be discussing soon. The ancient Hindu texts of the Upanishads are the texts to consult if you are curious about more detailed information on the Hindu side of things. This is not a Hinduism treatise, so I will proceed ahead full steam.

Elegant as they are, they can still be very fragile things, and thus it is wise to maintain as much diligence and attention to the energetic form as is paid to the physical form. Underdeveloped chakras can have undesirable consequences, and overdeveloped chakras can have the same, so it would be wise to develop a relationship with your energetic body as you would your physical form. There are many different ways to do this, ranging from various energy manipulation techniques like Reiki to gemstone balancings that use semiprecious stones to

---

[3]http://www.colorado.edu/religiousstudies/TheStrip/features/thesis/academics/avalon/wood1.htm

accomplish the same thing. A gemstone balancing is a technique that is fairly new, and in short, it is the laying on of stones at particular places on the body and/or around it. The stones emit vibrations, so the best example to think of is being energetically bathed in the stones and the energy they produce. Other than these energy driven techniques, good old fashioned physical exercise should also be used, particularly in conjunction with yoga, to strengthen the chakras and to keep the flow of energy stable and equal throughout the body. Using physical techniques can be seen as a sort of preventative measure, with the energetic techniques being an adjunct to the health process. By paying attention to the physical form as much as the energetic form, you put yourself in a position to attune to the spirit world to a greater degree than others. You truly do learn how to maximize your gifts of working with spirit.

Now this doesn't necessarily mean that everyone should go out and become a vegetarian for a number of reasons, but it does mean that you should pay attention to diet and all things related to taking care of health. As an extension of this, you should be aware that when you are sick with illness of any type, you should avoid doing spirit work unless absolutely positively necessary. There is a time and tide for everything, and sometimes that time is taking care of ourselves first and foremost. Other than the basic dietary considerations, there are a few key ones to keep in mind when dealing with spirits. To begin with, when you are preparing to do the work, it is wise to drink plenty of water for a substantial amount of time beforehand to flush the system, so to speak. This length of time varies from tradition to tradition, but I will use the model that is present in the western tradition that is based on traditional magic. In many places over the centuries, it has been said that any consumption of food or drink should occur no sooner than three hours before the time of the ritual. This is a good rule of thumb to follow, not only for the physical side of digestion, but also as a good starting point to begin drinking water. Yes, I realize this is a slight contradiction to what I said above, but also as I said, the three hour rule is more of a rule of thumb anyway. Usually, I don't eat anything substantial within three hours prior to a spirit working, whenever possible, but I drink water up until right before the event. I do listen to my bladder though, so stopping when appropriate is wise. If you are uncomfortable for digestive reasons when you sit down to do spirit work, then it lowers the quality of the manifestation of said work. By withholding food for the three hour window mentioned above, we dodge the whole question of whether or not to be vegetarian. This dietary topic has been hotly debated for a long time, so I wish to steer clear of it, but I will chime in on one point, which is the fact that red meat is a type of food that is meant to ground a person after spirit rapport has been achieved. Part of this point also addresses the fact that a person that eats more meat than someone that doesn't eat meat at all, like a vegetarian, is someone that is more grounded in the physical world, but this also keeps their vibration denser, so it's a fine line to walk to find the right dietary balance, and it is one that is ultimately subjective, once a dietary health care professional has been consulted.

Nadis and Kundalini

Everything comes back to energy, and thus let us turn our attention to the energetic flow and how chakras play an important role in this. While chakras are an integral part of the movement of energy through the etheric double, they are not the only part. Another part of this structure is that of the "nadis" (pronounced "nah-dees."). It's a Sanskrit word that means "tube" or "pipe," and this gives us immediate information as to what they are and what function they serve. Nadis are basically channels that the energy in the etheric body moves through as it circulates through the etheric double. This doesn't mean that the energy *only* flows through the nadis, but rather these are conduits. An excellent example to illustrate this idea is the well documented ley lines that exist across the planet Earth. These lines do not represent all of the energy, but rather they are simply the vessels through which strong energy flows. Channels that guide water, whether it's a river or a small stream, is a more tangible example. Anyhow, these channels, or nadis, run throughout the entire human aura in particular patterns that are rooted in sacred geometry. Nadis are evenly and rhythmically placed throughout the aura in symmetrical patterns that can be dissected to a very large degree, and interpreted on esoteric levels that command books of their own.

There are thousands of nadis throughout the human body, and since they're not systematically analyzed, it is impossible to go through all of the details here. However, we can still address a lot of information. For starters, these nadis can almost be thought of as energetic veins, which means we can use our concentration skills to direct the flow of energy to where we see fit, and by developing energy manipulation skills we can use this to greater effect. The second point to note is that nadis vary in size and conductivity. There are three major nadis that are commonly known among energy workers and they are worth noting here at least in passing so that we can understand the full range of potency that they have.

The first one to pay extra attention to is the Sushumna. This is a vertical nadi runs up parallel to the spine, and is the main conduit of two major energies: the Ida and Pingala. In order to understand them, it is wise to understand kundalini.

Before we get into kundalini, let's talk about energy itself. The concept of energy is known by different names in different cultures, but the essence is the same. Some could say this is the concept of the breath of life. In Chinese medicine this is Qi, and in Hinduism this is known as prana. Energy is energy, and is the foundation of everything we know of in reality. It is more than just wind, per se, but rather it is the very essence of what is carried on the wind. Some Hindu traditions even break this down further, into two types of energies, the lunar and the solar. These are known as kaulas, and while they are too extensive to embrace in this text, they are worth noting because it gives further insight into the universal laws of polarity and gender. I address this here simply for the sake of completeness, but if you are interested in knowing more about this, there are several good books that address the kaulas in depth, so it is easy to work with them. This is also true of prana and Qi, as they are well documented in both modern and ancient texts. An easy idea to use to work with energy in day to day life is to know that light equals energy. Hence, if you want more energy in your life, bring more light into it. On a practical level this could mean spending more time outside, and on a personal level this could simply mean wearing lighter colored clothes. I'm sure you get the idea to apply it to your own life. Anyway, back to kundalini.

Kundalini rests at the base of the spine, dormant. Arthur

Avalon coined the term "serpent power" to describe the energy in the late 19th century. This is an apt term for it, as the energy that lies dormant there can awaken like a dragon and be very fiery when used. At this nexus point at the base of the spine, the etheric energy used during sex waits to be used. While it may lie dormant, it can also be controlled and used for manifestation. Kundalini energy travels up this column as it arises and activates.

However, the energy doesn't just flow straight up, but rather there is a pattern to how it moves that is critical to understand. This is because there are two kinds of kundalini energy. Rather, there is a duality to kundalini energy to be aware of. Kundalini energy is both masculine and feminine. Each one has a particular color to it, and each one addresses what they say they do. For example, someone that has too much masculine kundalini energy will tend to be more aggressive. The root of each of these energies is the buttocks region of the body where they lie dormant. The left buttock is where the female energy flows from, and its name is "Ida." The right buttock, by extension, is where the male energy flows from, whose name is "Pingala." The way that they travel up the sushumna is that they crisscross much like DNA or Hermes' caduceus. The crossing over points occur in between the chakras, and when the energy gets to the base of the skull, the two energies cross again and come back down the head, exiting through the nose openings, Ida through the left, and Pingala through the right. By knowing how all of this flows, we can work on varying levels of control through practice and discipline. There are also a few correspondences to know as well that can assist us in visualizing the energy. Ida is said to be of a light electric blue color, and corresponds to Venus, while Pingala is said to be of a deep electric red color, and corresponds to Mars. The reason that the energy rests at the base of the spine has to do with nexus points of etheric nerves that are located throughout the body.

In addition to the energy discussed above, and the systematic analysis of the human energy form, there are a couple of other points to know. The first one is an energy field that radiates out from the heart. This used to be a concept that solely existed in metaphysics, but recently scientists have discovered that this is actually true on a quantifiable level.

The Heart Field

The common idea is that there is a very strong electromagnetic field that radiates out from the heart, and due to this, much bigger results can be achieved if one works with a heart centered life. There is an energy field that radiates out from the heart and helps to produce the energy field that comprises the aura, which we will discuss in a moment. In the last few years there has been a lot of research into this area, and as technology advances, we can expect more research on this to come to light. In short, it radiates out from the heart stronger than almost any other field in the body, including the field emitted from the brain. Existentially, this reveals a greater power of emotions than one may expect, but on a more practical level, this reminds us that if we are emotionally unhealthy, it can be detrimental to the body and to life itself. Numerous studies over the last few decades have spoken of the necessity to be emotionally healthy and in this way we can see research and science intersecting with metaphysics.

As each chakra spins, it produces energy, and as the heart beats and emotions are handled in a very positive and proactive way, an energy field is produced as well. Thus we can see that the two work in tandem to produce an energy field of a human being. We hinted at this above, but it is worth remembering here because it lets us know that the etheric double is multifaceted when it comes to how energy is produced, which also means it is multifaceted when it comes to manipulating said energy. In other words we can work with the chakras or the heart center to produce changes in our energy field, or we can work with both. Yes, in the earliest form of the chakra system, the heart is listed as one of them, which means that all three original chakras are powerful in their own rights, but when we take special note that the heart produces its own energy field in addition to the communal energy field produced by the chakras, we find more emphasis on the role of the heart in not only a biological context, but also on an emotional level.

The Aura

The aura is an energy field generated from several points in the etheric double, and the concept of the aura has been written about in so many books that I really don't see a reason to tread old ground here, other than just mentioning a few points that are necessary to understanding the mechanics of it, and especially how it relates to the spirit world and spirit communication.

The aura is an energy field that is generated from two sources: the chakras and the heart. As the chakras spin, energy is produced, and this energy is coupled with the energy that radiates from the heart center to produce the aura. As you can see, I'm keeping this a basic primer for a few different reasons. The first reason is because as I mentioned above, there are several different chakra systems out there, so I leave it to you, dear reader, to use your discretion, as there is no right or wrong system, but rather different traditions. I'm not certified in any one particular chakra system out there, so as the saying goes, I really don't have a dog in the fight. What I do care about, though, is in giving you this information so that you can make an informed decision no matter what you decide. Secondly, there is a lot of information already in print about all of these topics, so to quixotically go after an all-encompassing approach (which I believe would be quite dry and potentially spiritually dis-comforting) would ultimately be droll and detrimental to the focus of this book. I would rather focus on the spirit world and spirits anyway, which I believe you would, too.

Thus the keys to take away from this chapter are simple: Chakras and the heart produce energy, which creates the aura of an individual. While the aura is not the soul, it can be seen as one step closer to the soul (if such an idea exists or makes sense!) than the physical form. This means it behooves us to work with the aura so that we can control our vibration. As we learn how to control our vibration, we then gain control over what entities we can reach. I'm not going to tell you one energy manipulation system is better than any other. Each spiritual paradigm has this concept, and it is best that your intuition leads you to the proper approach for you. The one key thing to take away from working with them is the ability to manipulate your energy to either raise *or lower* it to connect with spirits. Yes, there, I went to dangerous ground. You see, in most channeling books out there, they will put the emphasis on raising your vibration to contact the highest vibration of spirits possible to bring through the clearest information possible. This is a point I wholeheartedly agree with! However, there are times when some people may want to lower their vibration for some reason or another to contact a lower vibrational spirit, so I mention this point here simply for the sake of wholeness. I do not suggest playing with this concept frivolously if you are at the beginner or even intermediate stage of development with your channeling techniques. This is something that only the advanced medium should contemplate, and even then, it may not be wise. I cannot stress enough the challenges and dangers that could potentially go along with this, especially long term use of such application.

Chapter 2: The Psychic Senses

In chapter one we discussed the human energy field and how to control and manipulate it, and now I would like to turn our attention to the senses that exist in the etheric double that we can use both in the spirit world and in the physical world. Sometimes this is known as ESP, or extrasensory perception, but it's the same thing, really.

ESP is a very broad, general term that is often used as a catchall to address any sense that is beyond the physical senses. This tells us by the very existence of the term that it is recognized there are senses that are known about that operate beyond the traditional five senses! I emphasize this because there are skeptics out there, and the existence of the term shows the validity of what we're discussing here. This is important to realize because when you are interacting with spirits and the spirit world, there is really not much room for self-doubting or second guessing yourself. Any sort of character defect like this produces doubt, which puts a cap on how extreme you can adjust your vibration, so it thus limits your growth. Analysis when dealing with spirits and the spirit world is key to continued growth in a controlled fashion.

It is my belief that everyone is born psychic, but this doesn't mean everyone is born with the same gifts or the same strength of gifts, but rather the strength and type of gift varies widely, based on many different factors, ranging from genetics to karma and soul experiences. It is very rare to find someone that is equally adept in all of the senses, and even when you do, this doesn't mean there is any spiritual enlightenment present. At this point it is necessary to interject some wisdom gained from experience: Just because someone is gifted with psychic senses **doesn't make them moral!** Spiritual development does not equal morally advanced, and so many times in the past I have met someone who claimed to be very spiritual, but all they had was an ESP skill or two and a dubious moral code. People commonly think two thoughts when they meet someone that has a psychic skill: 1) the person must be very spiritually advanced as a person, and/or 2) this skill is some sort of mystical gift. Let's get a couple of things straight. Having a strong ESP skill is nothing different than, say, being ambidextrous. It's simply a skill set. I have met many, many people over the years that are very adept when it comes to ESP skills, but are pretty much shitty human beings. As a matter of fact, helping people to protect themselves from people like these is something I put a lot of emphasis on, which also ties into my practical approach to metaphysics. I have also met very advanced people that don't manifest much in the way of ESP skills, so it works both ways. The ESP skills one has during this incarnation is the result of personal development work done in previous lifetimes, and it is because of this that there are so many variances regarding manifestation of said skills. This doesn't mean that the soul spent copious amounts of time developing the skill, but rather it can be a natural unfolding of personal development, and is a natural evolution of the human species. The more we evolve as a species, the more these abilities will unfold in a greater number of people. Evolution brings with it more intense skills for us as a species, so more people will have stronger gifts of varying types. It's simply science.

The idea that psychic skills are "gifts from god" is an idea that is tied to the dominant spiritual paradigm of approximately the last two thousand years, which is the Abrahamic belief system. In that spiritual paradigm, abilities beyond the normal were seen as either curses or gifts meted out from supernatural sources rather than being looked at as skills to be developed. Hence, you could argue that ESP skills are gifts, but that would predominantly be a thought from that belief system, as the concept removes the concept of personal power. By saying they are gifts from some all-powerful omnipotent being is also to say that you can't develop these on your own, which is pretty self-defeating, really, and disempowering overall. I prefer to be self-empowered, and to know that if I choose to develop an ESP skill I already have, then I am exercising to develop a skill I have, which is as natural as developing any other skill. To me, that's just a logical thought process, especially since we are moving into an age of increased science and reason.

The first step to developing your psychic skills is cultivating your awareness. This sounds broad, and perhaps even daunting, but this is the best way to expand your senses beyond the physical. There are two points I will share with you here that aren't necessarily exercises to work with, but rather concepts to ponder and to put into practice. The first one is a simple emphasis on being aware of everything you possibly can in your surroundings. At first, begin on a small scale with your immediate space, whether it is a room you are currently in, or perhaps the floor of a building. Focus on all five of your senses, and take an inventory of what you smell, what you may taste, and what you can see with your physical eyes. At this point, start with the extension of your five senses. After you have been doing this for a while and have gotten good at it, open your awareness to what you ~sense~ rather than experience with your senses. The more you practice situational awareness, the more you push the boundaries of what you can sense. The next point to be aware of is that oftentimes spirits will visibly manifest out of your peripheral vision. After you've cultivated situational awareness like we mentioned above, turn your awareness to specifically your periphery. If you see flicks of light in your periphery, you are seeing spirits, at least on a fundamental and rudimentary level. If you keep these two concepts in mind during your psychic unfolding, you may find you meet with greater success overall, and may even get faster results.

Intuition

One of the best places to start when it comes to developing your finer skills is to begin with your intuition, and thus I will begin with this one since it is relatively easy to develop. The best way to think of intuition is to think of it as your "gut response." Hence intuition is that instinctive impulse we all have. Where does it come from, and what can we do with it? Oftentimes it has been said that intuition is your raw, primal gut response that seems to "know" when there is no logical reason to "know." Some people say this is the sixth sense, but we'll discuss that idea in a few pages. Intuition comes from the subconscious mind, and oftentimes it is seen as an impulse of sorts. Some people call it a first reaction, and this is as close to true as there can be. This should be looked at a little bit closer though, to increase the understanding of what this means.

The human body is over 70 percent water, and water is a

conduit of energy. This also means that the human body is influenced by the same forces that affect oceans, streams, and other bodies of water. This is why the moon has as big of an impact on the human form as it does on the tides of the ocean. The human body responds to vibrations due to the common element of water, and without getting into too much technical talk here, the short part of it is that the body picks up on impulses that are subtle and invisible to the naked eye. Hence it knows a lot of things that we don't consciously know. This has been discussed in many books over the years, and I see no point to address it here, but it is worth mentioning for the sake of completion. Because there is no filtering from the conscious mind, it gets undiluted information, and only some of it comes to us through conscious thoughts and means. Of course this also gives weight to the idea of staying hydrated on the physical plane, which brings things full circle to "making sure you drink plenty of water," like I'm pretty sure we were all taught as children!

The human form works a second way, though, and this is because we can get to know our subconscious through interpreting impulses and messages from our body. Metaphysics has covered this extensively, but I will hit a few key points here to assist you in developing your own rapport with your physical body. Here are a few examples to illustrate: If you have a problem with one of your feet, then this can either mean you're on the go too much or not enough, depending on the nature of the physical condition. If there is a heart problem, this could mean that there are situations in the emotional body to address and heal. Occam's razor should also be applied here. Sometimes a heart problem or a foot problem is the result of genetic situations that are the result of karma from past lives, so dealing with them in this life is part of personal development. I mention this because sometimes the most obvious solution is the correct one. As you might expect, this also means you should *never* neglect the physical side of life. There is no difference between the spiritual world and the physical world after all, as they are intrinsically tied together, the spiritual world almost like a cloak or backdrop that the affairs of this planet play out against. It's not as hard as you may think to work with this concept, and I will give you ideas here. The idea that is easiest to work with is to understand the function of the particular body part to understand its metaphysical meaning and message. Feet are what we move forward with, hands are what we create with, the head is what we use to think, etc, etc, etc. I hope these are enough examples to guide you down a particular train of thought so you can assess your own body and what it may be telling you at this time, if anything. By listening to the language of the body, you are listening to the language of the subconscious, and in this way you are cultivating a closer relationship to your mind than many other people will accomplish. So the general flow here is: Your intuition comes from your subconscious, and your body is your subconscious mind. Therefore, ultimately, your intuition has its roots in your body. By addressing your diet and exercise, you improve your subconscious and can create positive change and personal growth firmly under your control. The way this applies to spirit contact should be obvious, but in case I haven't made myself clear, let me summarize: As you communicate with your subconscious, you increase your skill with your intuition. As you cultivate that relationship, you begin to create greater clarity with regards to the messages you receive. With this greater clarity, you raise your vibration by doing nothing more than improving yourself.

The key to putting intuition to work for you is to listen to your gut, but lead with your head. Too many times I have seen people throw common sense out the window in pursuit of manifesting the intuitive impulse, and this should almost never be the case. Yes, you should listen to your intuition because the information is unfiltered by the conscious mind, but this does not mean you should forgo planning, analysis, or forethought. Yes, follow your heart, but lead with your head with a plan that can be logically followed and applied. In order to do this easily it means that we should eventually develop to the degree that listening to intuition is seen as factual as the concept of eating satiating hunger. Not everyone is confident in their intuition, and because of this there is no one size fits all technique to cultivating your relationship with your intuition on a greater level. In my experience I have found that cultivating the relationship with your intuition is a trial and error process that takes time and mental fortitude to accomplish, and since it is a highly intimate relationship, it is also one that is highly subjective, so use your best judgment when it comes to cultivating this. Quick research can produce a substantial amount of material to work with, so other than a few exercises I will share here, there should be no shortage to use.

Exercise #1

The point of this exercise is to learn how to trust yourself. To begin with, think of a situation in your life that currently has you vexed. Quiet your mind, and ask yourself what is your first impulsive thought about the situation? Yes, the cynic will think something base and lower, and usually instantly gratifying, but seriously, *honestly*, what is your first impulse about it? Now that you have the answer to that question, ask yourself what it takes to manifest it. This is the step that can be tricky because it usually involves planning and forethought, mixed with the correct application of resources. This is a necessary step though, because planning is key to success in many things in life, and intuition is one as well. A secondary part of this step is to weigh two key factors: risk vs reward, and the return on investment (ROI). Is it worth it, and if it's not, then what is the meaning of the impulse? Sometimes we get impulses that we think we understand, but only to discover later we were wrong in our interpretation. The impulse we receive is simply an impulsive guide, but what we do with that information is up to us.

For those of you that may be feeling hesitant about taking this step, rest assured this doesn't have to be a huge situation that is currently vexing you. In other words, you could start with something small as a test subject before moving up to more intense subjects. I usually recommend this concept to people that may be grasping this material for the first time. It is truly the safer of the two ways to proceed. By working with the microcosm of a small situation, we come to understand the principles and energetics behind the situation itself. To borrow a concept from the occultist Dion Fortune, "examples may become outdated, but the principles remain the same."

Exercise #2

Take a mental tally of a physical situation you may be currently be working through, and if you're not facing any right now, congratulations! Not only does this mean you're healthy, it also means you are in tune with your subconscious, so you are less likely to experience unexpected eruptions from your subconscious that may self-sabotage you. This also means that you can skip this exercise and can refine your skill with the first exercise until you have it down pat.

When you think of that particular health situation, analyze what it's telling you. Apply real world functions of the body to the metaphysical. The examples listed above having to do with the body are to be contemplated, but here are a few other correspondences to consider. The lungs have to do with air, correct? In this case, air has to do with the breath of life, so challenges with the lungs may have to do with not feeling truly alive or connected with the spiritual side of life. Another idea to consider are the eyes. This introduces another concept into the equation which we will discuss in the next paragraph, but for now it is wise to focus on the fact that the eyes help us to see, so if there are challenges that have to do with the eyes, it is telling us there is a situation in our life that we are not seeing clearly.

There is one thing that should be known at this point, and that is that the human body is, for the most part, symmetrical, or at least in perfection it is. Metaphysics breaks this into halves, for lack of a better term. The dominant side of the body corresponds to the mental plane, while the other side of the body corresponds to the emotional plane. If you are perfectly symmetrical and ambidextrous, this tells us you are using both hemispheres of your brain in an almost equal amount, finding synthesis between the two and what they provide for us. Let us say that you are right handed and having problems with your right eye. This tells us there is something you are not seeing from a clear, logical, mental perspective. There is something in your life that could use some logic, reason, and analysis. However, if it is the left eye that has a problem, then this tells us there is an emotional situation that you are not seeing clearly. I hope this makes sense enough for you to start working with these concepts. There is so much more to what I've shared here that volumes could and have been written about this, so for the earnest student, much information can be obtained. I encourage you to work with intuition as a building block to further ESP skill development.

Let us now proceed to the rest of the skills that are out there and take a look at them in closer detail. By developing intuition and learning what skills you have, and to what degree you have them, you are creating a clearer channel for spirits to contact you, and for you to hear what they have to say. With this, I introduce you to the clairs. The clairs are accurate terms for the senses that we have and can use to interact with the spirit world. In this context, the term clair is from the French language, and in it, "clair" means "clear." Thus when you say clair-anything, you are saying "clear-" whatever. These terms originated between the latter 17th century and the mid-19th century. This time period is particularly noteworthy because it encompasses pivotal movements in our species' history, ranging from the Christian mysticism movement to the French Occult Revival, which paved the way for the modern expansion of occultism.

Clairvoyance

Instead of addressing these in alphabetical order, I am going to address the ones that are most commonly known and talked about, and because of this, I would like to start with clairvoyance, since this is what most people initially encounter when they begin to develop the psychic skills. The term can be broken down into "clear sight," and thus we get a clue to the concept over the centuries. Through time, it has been known as the second sight, the gift, and simply, the sight. This is also the most common psychic skill that has been recorded through history. Stories of people with "the sight" or "second sight" are rife in most cultures and spiritual traditions, and any time that you've read a story that addresses someone that is gifted with the power of prophecy, you have encountered clairvoyance.

Clairvoyance produces spirit sight, and comes from the pineal gland. This is a gland that is located in the forehead, specifically right above the eyebrows, and is a vertical placement. By stimulating the pineal gland, you can increase your spirit sight. It is part of the endocrine system and produces melatonin, which can help the body in many different ways. Interestingly enough, fluoride calcifies the pineal gland, stunting its growth.

It is clairvoyance that allows one to physically see spirits from the spirit world. Some people can see spirits as clearly as they can regular people in day to day life, and this is the result of a strong pineal gland. There's not a lot more that I can chime in with here that hasn't been discussed ad infinitum, so I will not attempt to cover trodden ground, but rather I will give you a few tips for working with your clairvoyance. To begin with, anything that has to do with melatonin and melatonin production can be very useful to integrate into your day to day life. Secondly, it would also be wise to watch your fluoride intake. Third, here is an exercise I give you to help stimulate your pineal gland.

Exercise #3

A very useful technique for developing your pineal gland is to get proficient at crossing your eyes. Yes, as silly as it sounds, this is actually a very useful technique to use for your personal development. Thus, step 1 of exercise 1 is to learn the ability to cross your eyes if you haven't already. Once you get this down pat, step 2 is to begin rotating your eyes upwards so it looks like your crossed eyes are looking at a spot that is slightly elevated outside of your normal field of vision and slightly above your brow. It may take a few times standing in front of the mirror to perfect this, but when you accomplish it, you have the full exercise to work with for as long as you notice results. As I discussed in *Vocal Magick* it takes the subconscious 28 days to learn a new pattern, so a conservative length of time before expecting results would be 28 days. I say this because there are those that may expect immediate results, and developing the pineal gland is not one of instant gratification. There is an addendum to this though, and that is that if you do notice faster results, you could interpret that as a sign that you have a natural affinity for it.

Clairaudience

This is the gift of clear hearing, so thus, this is the ability that has to do with hearing messages from the spirit world. For example, any time that you thought you heard words from a discarnate source, you were using clairaudience. Oftentimes people will hear their name, turn and look, and not see the source that produced it. The easiest way to process this is to understand that the source of the sound was in the spirit world, reaching across the veil to contact you. Your ability to discern where sounds are coming from can be very helpful not only to increase your psychic skills, but also because it puts us more in touch with the world we inhabit.

Exercise #4

While I have this listed under the clairaudience section of the chapter, it could just as easily be used for any of the clairs. Momentarily block one or more of your senses, and leave it that way for a specified period of time. By default this means it would be wise to be in a safe environment when you perform this. This is based on the premise that when one sense is weaker than the others, or damaged to the point of being ineffectual, the other senses compensate for its absence. This can be used to increase your psychic skills in the beginning using the tip I give you in this section. By temporarily turning off a sense or two for a brief period of time, you increase the potency of your psychic skills. I have found this very useful over the years because it enhances total awareness for when you're dealing with spirits because not all spirits communicate the same, and the circumstances of spirit contact may be such that only one of your psychic skills can be used, so it is wise to have them as sharp as you possibly can.

Clairsentience

This is the skill of clear feeling, but there is some explanation that will follow to clarify! Clear feeling is ~feeling~ a situation out to get a sense of what is happening on an energetic level. This can be seen as extending your senses out to get in touch with foreign energetics and beings in your close proximity.

At this juncture it is wise to clarify a common misunderstanding, which is that feelings and emotions are interchangeable. I feel this is important to note because, well, it's something I've had to clarify countless times. Your emotions come from within, and like we discussed above, emotions tie into the body and the element of water very strongly. However, *feelings* are actions. It's in the word itself. When you run your hand across a smooth surface, you are feeling with your fingers. When you walk, you are feeling with your feet and your toes. Having a feeling is interpreting an impulse from an external source. If it was an internal source, it would be your intuition. As elementary as this sounds, it is important to realize this to keep your critical thinking skills sharp. The further we get into this book, the more important it is to keep this in mind to prevent losing yourself in spiritual fantasy rather than spiritual reality. Staying grounded when you are working with spirits is something that is paramount to success. Too much work with spirits can make you unhealthy in a number of ways, but too little contact can also be detrimental to long term growth. Anyway, back to clairsentience.

Clairsentience is the only one of the clairs that could be considered the true, actual, sixth sense. It is that feeling you get when a spirit is near. It is that sense of feeling something present in the room with you. When you simply *know* something to be present, you are working with this skill. If you've ever felt a shiver go down your spine when you've walked over a grave, or have felt like you've accidentally walked through a ghost in a room, you've experienced this skill in action. Some people say that the temperature drops in the room when there is a ghost present, but I would like to put this on the back burner for the moment because I plan on going more in depth with this later in the book, but I mention it here because there may be some of you that had that idea at this point, and I would just ask you to table that thought for now.

The term psychometry often comes up when it comes to this particular skill, and this is partially true. Psychometry is the ability to touch a physical item and receive impressions regarding energetics attached to the item. So, for example, if you touch a statue of a deity, you can tell whether it was from the country of origin, or if it was manufactured elsewhere. If you touch a ring someone routinely wears, you may see details about them as accurately as you see the person sitting next to you at the dinner table. The easiest way to think of this is that it is the more physically plane tuned dimension of this skill.

Exercise #5

This exercise requires a partner, but the partner doesn't have to be a human. Find a quiet room where you won't be disturbed, and inhabit the room with your partner. Find a comfortable spot, seat yourself, and close your eyes. Breathe deeply to relax and let your senses pick out where your partner is in the room. If your partner is a human, ask them to do the same. If your partner is a pet, energetically track its movements (if any) through the room. As you can deduce, you can add more beings to the exercise and energetically locate and track them all. You can extrapolate this exercise almost ad infinitum to include different types of partners and different environments both inside and outside. A fun extension of this is to include plants as well as people and animals, and I encourage you to explore this exercise as you see fit.

Claircognizance

Clear-knowing is what this skill addresses. This is that simple knowledge of something to be true and in line with your spiritual development. This can oftentimes be misinterpreted as intuition, and there is only a fine line difference between the two. I will give hints and pointers for you to work with so that you can find the fine line for yourself. This is the psychic skill that could be seen as the perfect blend between the rational mind and the intuitive heart. Interestingly enough there's not a lot to be said about this psychic skill because this is the kind of knowing that can be hard to put into words and convey to others, so I'll just jump straight to the exercise.

Exercise #6

This exercise may take more hard work than the previous exercises, and it may be one that you come back to from time to time, so if you find yourself coming back to this over time, that is quite normal. The first step to work with this is to quiet your mind and enter into a Zen- like state of consciousness where you have dispersed with the barrier between you and the concept of the other. This is very similar to embracing the idea that we are all one. Usually I shy away from working with that concept because it can be too easily diluted, but when it comes to dealing with spirits and the spirit world, knowing that we are all part of an energetic whole field is critical to success because it allows you to fine tune your vibration to a greater extent. When you have reached the dissolution of this barrier, ask yourself a spiritual question that has been vexing you for a while. Now stretch to feel and simply *know* the appropriate solution. Most likely you will not be able to rationally explain your thought, but you simply know how to proceed. When you know, you can then let your intuition guide you as to how to achieve success in manifesting it in your life.

Clairsalience

This one and the following one are at the bottom of the list because they are two that are not discussed much, but still exist and can be developed. This particular sense is clear smelling. Yes, this is the psychic skill that has to do with smelling things that don't have a cause in the physical world. Have you ever walked into a room and smelled flowers that remind you of someone special, or perhaps a cologne unique to a loved one? Any and all of these have to do with clairsalience. This is particularly worth noting because researchers have determined that scent is the sense that is most associated with memory, which is one of the reasons why those phantom smells trigger memories of loved ones already in spirit. This is the most common experience someone has, so the likelihood of this having happened to you or someone you know is high from a probability perspective. Thus the exercise for this sense is pretty easy.

Exercise #7

Focus your senses on the smells that are in your particular space. It would be wise to start off conservatively, like your room or your home. Identify the scents and where they are coming from.

As you work with this skill, increase the number of scents you are exposed to incrementally to sharpen your skill. Once you get comfortable and successful doing this in your home, begin venturing out to public areas at your own discretion. Besides sharpening your sense of smell, it also sends the message into the universe that you are open to receiving scents from the spirit world.

Clairgustance

It has been my experience this is the most obscure of the clairs, and it is clear taste. Yes, such a skill actually exists, but quite honestly I don't know a lot about it because I have not encountered a lot of people that are skilled with this. The most common manifestation of this that I have heard from many people over the years is that when they tune into a past life, they can taste tastes that are associated with that memory. Hence if this is true, we can infer that this is also true for messages from the spirit world.

Exercise #8

Think of memories that you have, that have particularly strong emotional attachments, and reflect on any tastes that may have been present. Begin to pay attention to your food and how it tastes. When it comes to drinking liquids, focus on the taste as it slides down your throat.

I realize this has been a brief introduction to the psychic skills, but I hope the exercises provide a pathway for you to explore your strengths and weaknesses to get a better sense of what you're good at, and how you handle your interactions with the spirit world. As you work through these exercises, remember to record your results in your journal. In addition to recording your results, record external factors such as the phases of the moon, planets that may be retrograde, the seasons, etc, to observe how these influence your work. This also concludes the first section of the book as well. Now we move onto an exploration of the spirit world. Now that familiarity has been established with the energetic self, we can enter into interacting with the spirit world on much firmer ground, more confident in our ability to interact with beings that some relegate to exclusively fantasy or delusion.

Part Two: The Spirit World

Chapter 3: The Planes

I don't really know what else can be said about the spirit world that hasn't been said before, but I will take this opportunity to share a view that is logical and makes sense to me. To the ancients there were seven wandering lights in the sky, and as a matter of fact, that is the root of the word "planet." They were seen as wandering because they moved across the sky as opposed to the fixed stars in the background. These wandering lights eventually became known as the planets in our solar system, and the seven that were recorded are: the Sun, the Moon, Mercury, Venus, Mars, Jupiter, and Saturn. Yes, there are theories out there that ancient people knew about more than just those seven planets, but that is irrelevant to our conversation here, and would require a book all to itself, so for now let's focus on the seven classical planets.

Well, not really. We're not really focusing on an in depth look at the planets, but rather simply recognizing that they were the seven lights of the ancients. As many of you most likely know, the number seven is sacred in magic and spiritual systems across the world. It has been known as the number of magic and the number of Venus, among other things, and the list of correspondences is lengthy, but suffice to know for now, it's an important number. The clearest scheme I have found to illustrate and delineate the spirit world free of dogma is that of seven planes and seven subplanes for each one. This makes sense because metaphysics teaches an underlying principle that is easy to work with, and that is that each planet represents a different plane of understanding and/or existence. An alternative to this is the five planes system in western occultism, but they are also interwoven into the seven plane model, so we will discuss them all by default. From time immemorial the stars have been gazed upon, and stories told of what they may be, so whether intentionally or not, they have influenced our concepts of the unseen world, so it's as good of a starting point as any.

If you noticed in the table of contents, there are five subsections in this chapter, but I've been discussing a seven plane model. Once we leave the mental plane and venture into the plane of spirit, things get trickier, so that particular section will be longer and more detailed, but will give clarification on the other two planes. The five subsections of this chapter correspond to the classical five elements used in Western traditional occultism today, and even that is arguable from a qabalistic perspective since the entirety of the four elements is relegated to Malkuth at the bottom of the tree, one sephiroth out of ten. I'm choosing a different approach here, but I want to mention this so that we're all on the same page. Yes, all four elements that we work with are only confined to the physical plane, and this is useful to keep in mind when thinking in terms of energy. The energy that we've been discussing is beyond the four elements, but their wisdom and insight can be used when it comes to dealing with spirits and the spirit world. Being familiar and experienced with the concepts of the elements gives greater control over your vibration when you contact spirits. If you can control your resonance to the degree you are harmonizing with traits of the elements, you are one step ahead when it comes to spirit communication. In the multiverse there are spirits of each element that you may come into contact with. Western occultism has addressed elementals and what these elements are, so here again I will keep my comments and remarks about the elemental kingdoms succinct.

A flaw in logic to avoid is that these are mutually exclusive places in some sort of time and space continuum. The planes overlap, and at first this may make things tricky when it comes to recognizing what plane you're working with, but with time and experience this gets a lot easier to use. In the spirit world, there are no concrete lines of demarcation, and the best way to think of this is that the spirit world is very similar to human society in that it is a sliding scale of grey, so as one plane dissolves, another one comes into manifestation. This also means that each plane itself ranges from being the stereotypical manifestation of said plane's correspondences to being partially influenced by the plane above or below it. Thus you can have a watery earth being in spirit that you're dealing with, and in a different context you may encounter a pure earth being. This is elegantly addressed in the Enochian system of magic, and it's simply worth knowing here because if you're interested in this tangent, that would be the direction to explore.

One final point to know before we start delving deeper into the planes is to address how we approach these planes. We live in a polarity based reality, and because of this we tend to look at things from a very head on approach, but this stubbornness is ultimately detrimental because it creates conflict when an easier approach can be had. Remember what I said earlier? The flow of energy through the cosmos is via the path of least resistance, so to create conflict when an easier approach is available is self-defeating. As Dion Fortune wrote, to paraphrase, to gain control of a plane, you approach it from the plane above it[4]. Therefore, if you have a physical plane issue that you're dealing with, it is wise to approach it from the emotional plane, which is the plane above it. If you have an emotional issue, then one of the worst ways to approach it is from an emotional perspective, but rather to approach it from a mental perspective. About the only time this isn't true is when it comes to the physical plane because it is the most condensed plane. For example, if you're overweight, then exercise and possibly diet are the solutions, but you may have to get emotionally invested in your goal to find the discipline to accomplish it. Thus you would be using the plane below the emotional, which is the physical, to accomplish emotional plane goals.

The Physical Plane

This is the easiest plane to work with and it is the one most of us interact with on a daily basis, and therefore, if we're doing anything right, it is the one we're the most successful at manipulating. The physical plane is the one we're all familiar with by default. We are all in physical form for many different reasons, and our individual beliefs on this subject are irrelevant to what we're talking about here because I would like to focus on what exactly the physical plane is. It is the world in which we live. It is everything we experience with our five senses, and

---

[4]Circuit of Force, Dion Fortune

because of this, it is the most documented of all the planes. Because of this I don't plan on spending a lot of time on it here, as this is best left to science and many other specialized fields of study. However, there are a few things I would like to draw our attention to in the name of clarity.

Everything in the physical world vibrates at a very low and slow vibration. The rule of thumb is that the denser the material, the slower the vibration. Yes, this means that everything in the physical world is vibrating, it's just that this is occurring slowly, and is a sliding scale as to how slowly something is vibrating. For example, metal is denser than wood, and is thus known to be vibrating at a much slower rate than wood. Plastic is more malleable and thus the vibration is higher than either wood or metal. I'm sure at this point you see where I'm going with this. Different kinds of materials have different vibratory rates. This is important for two particular reasons: 1) This means nothing is truly solid, but rather everything is in a semblance of motion at least, and 2) the slower the vibration, which also means the denser the material, the longer and more intensely it holds an impression. If you touch an item that is metal, you will be tapping into energies that are much older and more ingrained than if you touch an item of wood. This is also worth paying attention to when you are performing any kind of energetic cleansing. For example, it may take more work to cleanse a piece of metal than it does to cleanse a piece of wood. Also, if you follow this line of logic through, it tells us it is wise to energetically cleanse every item that comes into your personal space, especially if it is something you bought secondhand. Impressions may still be attached to the item from the previous owner, and thus you may unintentionally succumb to the effects of the impressions without realizing it. For example, if you buy a chair at a secondhand store, and all of a sudden you notice you start drinking more alcohol (this is extreme for the sake of clarity), and there is no other reason for this, it may be due to the fact that the chair was previously owned by an alcoholic. With thought you can easily extrapolate this out to your own particular situations you may encounter as you personally develop.

There are also a few cosmic facts to be mindful of when looking at the physical universe as well as the terrestrial world.

The first is that we are all composed of stardust and star matter. Yes, there are many qualifiers to this basic concept, but like I said, keep this in mind when working with the spirit world because it assists in the control of one's vibration in a more finely tuned manner. This is a subtle concept, and because of this it oftentimes falls into our subconscious, returning only infrequently. Therefore, the exercise that goes with this concept is to take time before every spirit working session to *feel* this energy inside you, and extend your senses to feel it around you, almost like electricity. A second cosmic point to be aware of is that it has been proven, at least to my knowledge, that there is more dark matter in our known multiverse than actual matter. This means what we experience with our five senses is relegated, at best, to experiencing only a small fraction of what is truly out there. This is one of the best justifications for being very discerning when it comes to identifying spirits you may come into contact with. Contrary to popular belief, not everything you will meet will have a name or categorization like you may think it should. There are things in the spirit world that very few people have met before, so you may not be familiar with them. There may also be spirits that were more common in certain ancient cultures that have now fallen into the haze of memory, all but forgotten to us, yet still autonomously existing on at least the next plane up, which we will address in a moment. At this point it is simply enough to know that our five senses, however sharp they may be, are still extremely limited in scope. They are some of my favorite senses, though, because it is this physical world that we have chosen to inhabit during this lifetime. We are here to experience what the world has to offer, and the education we glean from attending this earth school. One final point, and to some this may sound grim, but everything dies. Yes, the two biggest initiations any of us have is our birth and our death. Death is simply another initiation into something new or unknown.

The Astral Plane

Ahhh, the astral plane. No plane of existence has been talked about as much as the astral plane, save the physical plane. Throughout the centuries and varied traditions across the globe, there have been many perspectives of this plane, and because of this, one thing we know immediately is that it is a plane of dynamic sights and experiences. However, also because of this, there is a great deal of misconception about what it is and what it isn't, and how to deal with it. I will therefore lay down a lot of detailed information to assist the person that is reading about this for the first time, and for the person that is hearing this material from me for the first time.

It has often been said in magical circles that the astral plane is that of the imagination, but that it is also that of an objective reality, so let's take a few moments to address this point before continuing a more detailed look at it. The astral plane is the plane of emotions, and hence whenever you engage in an act that gets your emotions stimulated, you are engaging on the astral plane. This makes the astral plane a subjective experience for each and every explorer. However, we as a species share some common visions or fantasies that stimulate the imagination. The first one that comes to mind is to become independently wealthy and to not have a care in the world. I think it's safe to say that almost anyone on the planet would love this to happen to them. Thus this concept exists on the personal subjective astral plane as well as the collective astral plane of the species. With thought, I'm sure common fantasies among people will come to mind, but if you want to explore further, get together with some friends and discuss fantasies. Then see how many of them are common in the group you are in, because this gives you an idea of other fantasies that may not be yours. Even though they may not be your fantasies, credence should be given to them on the same level as yours, and hence we see that all of us, together or individually, create the astral plane all the time. This also means that the astral plane is a very fluid place with a shifting landscape and shifting entities that can be found there.

Dr. Carl Jung gave us the best term to use when looking at the astral plane when he brought the phrase "alchemical imagination" into mass consciousness and use. This is precisely what the astral plane is and how it can be used. This is a point that is oftentimes talked about in metaphysical and ancient wisdom circles, and working with this concept can produce many powerful results. In short, we come full circle back to my first book *Vocal Magick* because a teaching in there is also true here, and that is the teaching of being in control of your thoughts and words. This also means being in control of your desires, fantasies, and visions, especially when it comes to your inner life. How we envision ourselves when it comes to our imagination gives us a lot of insight into who we truly are, and thus we learn about ourselves by seeing where our imagination goes during times of joy, pleasure, stress, and anger. These may seem like seemingly disparate concepts, but as I stated above, anything that gets the emotions stimulated can lead you to the astral plane very quickly. If you want different results in your life, then it is wise to work with your imagination in a different way, because your inner life determines your outer perceptions. This can be a tall order to fill, though, as anyone that has tried to change their perspective on something knows, and thus we find that the easiest way to approach this is from the mental plane of logic, reason, and all things related to clear thinking and the left hemisphere of the brain. Through detachment we find ourselves empowered enough to wrangle control of our subjective astral plane and to put it to work for us. The astral plane is truly the furnace of the alchemical imagination because this is where we forge our desires, thoughtforms, and other parts of our psyches. This is where we dream, but this is also where we have nightmares. Each of us has an astral plane, and through commonly shared fantasies and desires this becomes objective and real.

Usually, the average person accesses it through creativity as mentioned above, but there is also a more direct route to access it, and that is the route of astral projection, which is sometimes called an out of body experience. This is a method that takes a lot more work than simply using the imagination and controlling your visions. This takes discipline and perseverance, since sometimes it can take a while until we find what method works best for us. There have been numerous books published on this technique throughout the years, so I won't cover trodden ground, but I will give you one technique to try in case this is your first experience with it. This technique is quite simple and common, yet also very effective.

Exercise #9

Take a playing card or tarot card, or really any card that can't be identified by its back. Make sure that your selection of the card is random, and draw it without looking at it. Keep its front image turned away from you, and place it some place high up in your house that you can't reach normally. Of course this means you'll need a stepstool or something similar, so make sure you have access to that, too. Without looking at the front, place it out of reach as mentioned above. Then, lay down on the bed on your back, close your eyes, and relax. Sometimes relaxing music helps with this. Other times silence may be perfect, so use whichever approach works for you. Imagine yourself leaving your body. The easiest way I can describe it is to imagine that you are getting out of your body while your physical body is still lying down. This is the part that challenges most people, so you may have to stick with it for a while before you get it down. The easiest channel to leave your body through is by exiting at the top of your head. There may be an energetic shock, and typically this is what pushes someone back into their body subconsciously, so if this occurs, there is no reason to get upset, but rather this is the best motivation to do it again when you've relaxed. After you get comfortable with getting out of your body, then begin to maneuver around the room. Yes, you are correct, that you can float walk, dance, etc, but most importantly you can take a look at the front of the card that you placed high up in the room. After you have accomplished this, return to your body and check the card to see if what you saw matches. Yes, sometimes in the beginning you may find you only get part of the card right, and yes, sometimes you may find the astral plane around you isn't what you expected at all, and both of these are quite okay. Repeat this method until you find a method that works better for you, or you achieve crystal clear success. Once you've mastered leaving your body, you can then begin to travel wherever you want, but I leave you to your own devices with that because from here things become tailor-made to your path.

As mentioned in the introduction to this chapter, the planes are not mutually exclusive, and this is worth pointing out here because when you leave your body, you are technically on a subplane of the astral plane. Clear as mud? Allow me to explain this breakdown because it took me a long time to make it clear for myself, and if this is the first you're hearing about the subdivisions of the astral plane, things may seem confusing or murky. For each plane there are seven subplanes, but none are as detailed as the astral plane. This is true for two very big reasons. The first reason is that this plane which is closest to the physical plane has been well documented over centuries through various cultures across history in depth, and all of these are true. Hence as belief systems and people have evolved, this information has continued to be refined, and as a capstone to it, the clairvoyants of the 19th and 20th centuries have brought increased clarity to the situation. This is why in this text you won't find each subplane of subsequent planes delineated; the information simply isn't there. However, I can go into detail about the astral, and we will begin our journey at the seventh subplane of the astral: the one that is at the bottom.

It is wise to remember the Hermetic Axiom at this point though: "As above, so below. As within, so without." While the astral plane is a location, it is also part of the internal landscape that we all deal with every day. Existentially, the astral plane corresponds to emotions, which means that this is occurring in our own consciousness as part of an ongoing part of spiritual evolution. For example, if someone comes from a very emotionally abusive background, they would, by default, start at a lower part of the emotional plane before they begin to develop themselves higher. This is neither bad nor good, but rather something that simply is, for a variety of factors, including karma and events that have happened due to free will choices by other people. As we all know, someone can choose to evolve higher and lower as they choose, through the consequences of their own actions. Hence this is not a static spot of development, but rather a starting point. For more information on this concept, please consult *Power Vs Force* by David Hawkins. This is simply worth noting here because it gives us insight into the dual uses of the astral plane: both for exploration, yet also internal development.

One final point to mention before moving on is that these subplanes can be seen as slowly moving farther out from the physical plane. The model of a cube in the middle with concentric circles moving farther away from it comes to mind here, and it would be wise to remember this if you plan on doing any astral exploring. This gives us part of a coordinate when it comes to the astral plane, and the internal compass gives us the other part of the coordinate. Through the control of your consciousness you can ascend the planes internally, and this translates to being able to handle more of an ascent through the concentric circles as they move away from the physical plane.

The lowest subplane of the astral plane is the seventh subplane, and the best description of this is the idea of the underworld. The backdrop of this subplane is usually that of the physical reality we all inhabit, but there is much less light, and let's not forget that light equals energy. In a lot of cultures this would be the idea of the underworld in all of its forms: Hel, the land ruled by Hades, etc. This lies beneath the surface as it were. These are the thickest, most condensed vibrations and beings that exist, and when something is said to be from the lower astral, this would be one of the subplanes that could be a strong possibility.

The sixth, fifth, and fourth subplanes of the astral are more what we would expect to see when we enter the astral realm. Like the seventh, the backdrop for these subplanes is the physical world that we inhabit, but the energies and vibrations are not nearly as condensed as they are in the seventh. As you can deduce, these three subplanes are varying shades of grey, and an excellent example of a denizen of one of these subplanes is a ghost. Usually ghosts are the cast off etheric doubles of people that went through a trauma at the time of their deaths. However, another leading cause for ghosts is the passion and desire created by the individual when they were alive, and now keeps them chained to a place, an item, or a person. Immediately after death they are more vibrant, but over time they slowly fade for a variety of reasons: the passion wanes, people forget about them, they don't know where to go, etc. As this waning process occurs, they begin to slowly fade out to further subplanes until reaching the fourth. The fourth subplane is the midpoint of the astral plane, and it is here that the battleground can be found. This battleground is the battle between the higher mind and the desire mind. The desire mind is the leftovers from the reptilian brain, and has to do with instant gratification and the fulfillment of base needs and wants. In a lot of ways this is a purging point, but it is also a point of coming to terms with what one is. This is the place where this is played out in cathartic detail. In this location, spirits are said to have their own homes and abodes, and that they create their reality in line with their vision, so this can be a very shifting landscape. Subplanes one, two, and three are the highest of the astral, and the easiest way to think of them is as the happy afterlives of so many belief systems.

This could be the Summerland from Spiritualism, or the heaven of the Abrahamic belief systems. The best indicator of whether or not an afterlife belongs here lies in the adjectives that are often used to describe it, and specifically these adjectives would address emotions invoked within the person that finds themselves there. This is also why this type of afterlife is spread across three subplanes. There are many variations of what can commonly be called "heaven," and they vary in many dynamic ways. The key point to know while figuring out what goes where is that by the time you get to the first subplane of the astral, you are as far out from the physical world as you can get, and you find yourself at the threshold of the mental plane. Interestingly enough, those same three subplanes of the astral are already showing an influence from the mental plane because all of them are the results of the desires of the practitioners, and thus address dedication, devotion, and discipline as ways to achieve this idea of salvation. By the time you get to the higher astral, the desire mind is reigned in and subjugated in favor of the human mind (as opposed to the animal mind). However, we all know that there are beings out there that may never leave the lower planes of the astral, and that is all well and good, but we should be on alert because they oftentimes do their best to take advantage of the unsuspecting. Thankfully though, these kinds of creatures are fading into our rear view mirror as we turn our attention to the next plane up and out: the Mental Plane.

The Inner Temple and the Astral Body

In classical magic it is taught that the first thing to do to move forward in magic is to develop your astral temple and work with your astral body. There are a few points of clarification to make that are extremely important to the process. The first point is that this means before you go deeply into magic, you must have things together on the physical plane to the degree that it is solid, stable, and consistent, so it doesn't have to be focused on at the expense of your spiritual growth. It's hard to be spiritually focused if you're constantly fretting about the physical plane.

But what is this astral temple? The astral temple is your sanctum sanctorum. It is your inner temple, your sanctuary, your seat of power, as it were. It is built on desires and dreams, as well as astral manipulation, and the best part is, no physical laws apply to it! That's right: it can look and feel however you want it! Imagination is the key here, and it is the only limit.

Exercise #10

To begin developing your astral temple, the first thing to do is to let your imagination run wild. Think about what you want it to look like, how you want it to smell and feel, and how you want to protect it. As you develop a clear picture of this, you can then move on to deciding who is allowed there and who isn't. Some people like to have their guides and teachers there, while others prefer it solitary. How you proceed with it is entirely up to you. The main point here is to take about 20 minutes a day to fashion it in line with your desires and Will. Also as an aside is that during this creation process it would be wise to leave no stone unturned, as it were. For example, are there wards of protection here? What about its permanency? Is it fluid, changing to your desires, or is it static, a rock you can build from?

The Mental Plane

We now come to the mental plane, which is the plane higher and farther out than the astral plane. This is the plane of the intellect. This is the plane of logic, reason, and abstract thought. While according to a lot of sources it is not as detailed out as the astral plane is, there are still a few things regarding its structure that we can take away from it and look at in a more thorough way.

The first concept to know is that the basic structure of the mental plane is the same, with a total of seven subplanes which are further split into three "groups." Subplanes seven, six, and five are the three lowest, four is where the middle ground/battleground is, and subplanes one, two, and three are at the high end of the mental plane.

But what does this truly mean? With the astral plane it's pretty easy to see, as the lower the plane, the more dense the energy and vibrations, but with the mental plane we find that the lower plane is the astral instead of the physical, so this does change things quite a bit. Because of this, the lowest subplanes, seven through five, are the densest of the mental plane, but their density only goes down as far as the astral plane and doesn't make physical plane contact. Because of this, the lowest three subplanes are known to address the concrete, logical mind. As I said earlier, the mental plane is the plane of the intellect, reason, and logic. It is rationale at its finest. However, this is not the totality of the mental plane, but rather broad characteristics of it. Science, mathematics, and all things related to hard logic and reason can be found on those lowest three subplanes. A good example of this is that person we all know that is so blinded by logic that they have atrophied their compassion. Of course the converse can be true, too, as we all know people that are more emotional than logical, but that would be someone on the astral plane, not the mental, but the principle is still in effect.

The fourth subplane that is the midway point or battleground, depending on your psychological disposition, is that of finding harmony and balance between these lower subplanes and the next three in the sequence. Subplanes one, two, and three have to do with abstract thought. When this is known, it becomes clear that the middle subplane is finding the balance between abstract thinking and thought vs concrete science and logic. Thus you can see there is no influence from the astral plane beyond what you would expect, which is the influence of intuition and the heart. As we take a more critical look at things, we find the "battle" that is occurring is between concrete logic and thought vs abstract thinking. Once someone gets too entrenched in logic and related concepts, they can get stuck in a form of dogma, and only by working with abstractions can they open their mind to what can happen. Oftentimes it has been said that all it takes for something to work is imagination, and that is a large part of the point here.

The Spiritual Plane

Again, at this point I don't know if much more can be said about the spiritual plane, especially since it has been written about extensively in the context of many worldwide spiritual traditions, so this section will be brief. However, there are a few things to pay special attention to in order to lay the foundation for the second half of this book. Because of the many billions of people that have worked with the spiritual plane globally over the last few thousand years, there is a very rich energetic history here that one can tap into and contact. While this is good due to the depth of information available, it can also be daunting to assimilate. However, something that the seeker has on their side is the fact that so much of this material is subjective and open to personal interpretation. While there are still the archaeological underpinnings that ultimately define the remaining facts of a culture, the way the information is interpreted and worked with is still largely up to the student.

Spirits work with us through the medium of what we know and because of this, it is wise to have a wide palette to work with and to use in order to establish better and more accurate connections. Thus it is wise to learn as much about the pantheons that you are drawn to as you possibly can. This helps refine your knowledge, but also gives spirits more to use in order to bring through clearer messages. Some people may take this to the extreme and use it for justification to learn as much as they can about everything. However, this is a bottomless pit, and is thus illusion. It is wise to pick a few favorite pantheons and to be highly familiar with them. Most people have one or two favorite pantheons to work with, but some have three or four. I have observed that once you get past the three pantheon limit, you really start to limit what you know because of breadth rather than depth. It is also important to note here that this refers to working with these pantheons, not just reading about them in a book. There are two sides to things: theory and practice, and while a lot of growth can be had from studying pantheons, just as much can be learned about incorporating certain facets of them into your daily life. There is a lot of freedom in this though, due to the fact that a lot of methods and practices from ancient cultures have not survived to the present day, and thus there is a lot that is open to interpretation. About the best rule of thumb to keep in mind is to keep a healthy perspective and clear context when it comes to working with them. For example, there are basic traits for the Norse pantheon that are not present in the Egyptian pantheon. By knowing general concepts and practices, you can increase your ability to work with these energies in a very living way.

Why is this important, you may be thinking? Well, the first reason is because beings from pantheons will be drawn to you more readily if you know their ways. While this is not a 100 percent set in stone fact, it is something to keep in mind because these practices create resonances, and through these resonances, a clearer and more controlled relationship can be established. Here's a generic example to illustrate the point: An ancient Egyptian entity will be drawn to you more strongly if you use oils in your methods of contact because oils were heavily used in ancient Egyptian ceremonies. The second reason this is important is because this daily behavior trains the subconscious, and as I described in *Vocal Magick*, when the subconscious is imprinted, it is easier to receive impressions from the spirit world than if the information is only available in your conscious mind. Your subconscious is the seat of power when it comes to working with spirits, and thus it is better to train it proactively than to have to deal with it reactively.

Another important facet of the spiritual plane is that of personal gnosis. Gnosis is an often misunderstood concept, so I will take a bit to explain it, but when working with the spiritual plane, it is important to be aware of, and to work with as you see fit. The first type of gnosis that exists is the type of gnosis that has descended from the Abrahamic belief system, and can be traced back to the Hellenistic period of Greece. This is a body of wisdom that is readily available today, and in a lot of ways it is a Western world version of Buddhism or Confucianism, bringing with it wisdom, compassion, and an almost intuitive sense with it. For those that are interested in it, there is a lot of material out there, so I encourage you to explore as you see fit.

However, the other type of gnosis that is out there is *personal gnosis*, which is wisdom received intuitively from the inner planes or the finer planes, depending on your preferred nomenclature. To illustrate, personal gnosis is what occurs when you contemplate or meditate on a topic and you receive very inspired wisdom and insight. Thus it comes from unseen sources, but when worked with, it has been proven to be correct. How to test the validity of the information, though, is the question. There are two ways that I have found to test this information. The first way is to research the information that has been received to see if it is information that is already known about or not. If it is, then there's your validation. You received something through reflection or meditation, and you were able to look it up to see that it already exists. Thus you learned something that existed without research. When that happens, I can assure you that it is very empowering. However, another way to check this information is to see if it lines up with the characteristics of the applicable pantheon. For example, if I received a message from a spirit in meditation who claimed to be Zeus, and it claimed to be celibate and pure, I would immediately know that spirit is not Zeus because I know the stories of Zeus, and thus I would know the spirit is a fraud.

I would like to interject a slight disclaimer here though, and that is that I test my spirits because I interact with a lot of them, and they really like interacting with me. This scenario will not be the case 80 percent of the time you channel, but rather this is the exception to the rule rather than the rule itself. It is generally uncommon for this to be a normal part of spirit contact, as usually the karmic law of attraction is in action, and the only spirits that are drawn to you are the ones that you share a common resonance with. In other words, if your vision and intention is pure, devout, and clear, then those are the types of spirits you will contact and that will contact you. However, as you grow and develop your spiritual gifts, your light will shine brighter on the other side of the veil, and this will draw many other spirits to you, but not all will be pure. Ever-vigilance is a concept to embrace, and discernment is the primary skill when working with the spiritual plane.

Chapter 4: Vortices, Sacred Sites, Ley Lines, Dragon Lines

The last few chapters have been focused on the individual, but there is a greater world out there, and in this chapter I would like to address it more in depth. As I have stated a few times, there is much more out there than what I could possibly write in this tome, so I share this information to be used as a beginning point for development rather than a be-all-end-all destination. When you begin to routinely work with spirits and have out of body experiences, you will discover that the spirit world is a rich tapestry that is almost constantly shifting, and because of this, it is the perfect example of the territory, not the map. I will give you guidelines, but ultimately the experiences will be yours and yours alone. There are a couple of interesting reasons for this. The first reason is that while there are humans alive on the planet, these planes will constantly be in motion due to the evolution of the species, and thus they are never static. The second reason is because of the blurred line between objective and subjective reality. I touched on this earlier when talking about the alchemical imagination, and that is worth remembering here. Each and every one of us is constantly evolving (if we're doing anything right!), and we are always energetically in motion. I have picked out a few key points to know when it comes to the spirit world and I will address them in this chapter. There are many more facets out there, and the blessing is that almost every spiritual tradition has a lot of information available on their interpretation of the spirit world, so you will most likely discover there is no shortage of resources.

Sacred Sites

Across the planet there are sacred sites that exist on the physical plane that usually tie into a culture and/or belief system in some way. Usually these are places that psychics would consider extra charged or particularly strong when viewed energetically. They generally have significance to the people that work within that spiritual paradigm, and oftentimes they are even seen as simply extra restful or peaceful by those that don't actively pursue their spiritual development. The Pyramid of Cheops comes to mind here as the best example, but there are many others: Stonehenge, Chaco Canyon, Glastonbury, and Angkor Wat, to name but a few.

Usually the sacred site is a place that corresponds to gods and/or goddesses in some form or another. Of course there are times that they are dedicated to many deities as well, or to some other purpose, such as Nabta Playa in Egypt. In more modern times they have corresponded to simply sacred places that were recognized by indigenous cultures before the dominant culture came into being. Temples are very interesting to pay attention to because they may have corresponded to a deity in antiquity, but now they are more general in nature. In contrast to this are shrines, which are usually sacred groves or grottoes, and are more likely to correspond to specific spiritual events.

Most of the time, these sacred sites are constructed rather than natural, but for the most part, the constructed part was placed on top of a natural vortex (also sometimes called a node), but we'll talk about that in the next section. However, they can also be a blend of the environment and construction, as is the case with the temple Petra, in Jordan, which is a sacred site constructed into the side of a cliff. You can usually identify sacred sites by the Euclidean geometric layout of the structure or structures. What recent scientific advancements have revealed is that they have been so carefully, strategically, and subtly created that we are still learning about them, their construction, and their significance. Now is the golden age for research that is being done into this area, as independent researchers are more empowered in their quest for truth due to recent advancements of technology. People are picking a favored area of interest and are devoting their lives to the research of that subject, so much more has been revealed in the last few decades than in the last century.

There is another side to this, though, and because we exist in a polarity based reality, what exists is the darker side of the equation. There are sacred sites that are also the locations of mass atrocities. Auschwitz comes to mind, as do some American civil war battlefields. As you can see, these sacred sites are places that were *created* by unspeakable and horrific acts. Thus it can be inferred that there are darker sacred sites than what are known about. We can research locations of mass murder, for example, but what about the cultures that didn't write much down, such as the Aztecs? This is important to note because it tells us there is really no way to account for all of the sacred sites that exist on the planet, but by learning the characteristics that go along with these sites, we can attune ourselves to their energetics if we find ourselves in their presence, if we choose to.

Vortices & Ley Lines

A vortex, or vortices, which is the plural form of the word, is a place where energy collects, and is in that way a nexus point for energy as it flows across the globe. These channels are known as ley lines, or alternatively, dragon lines, and they can be seen as the energetic wiring of the planet. Energy flows in a concentrated fashion through these lines, and the best parallel image to apply to these are pipes or conduits. The major difference between pipes/conduits and ley lines is that the energy that flows isn't confined by any external structure, so rather you find that the energy sometimes ripples out into the immediate area rather than being confined to rigid definitions. What is very interesting to note is that ley lines across the globe are laid out in a symmetrical way that is tied into sacred geometry. There is a geometry and a symmetry to these energetic lines, and thus it shows an intelligent design present. This isn't the intelligent design that is talked about regarding creation though, but rather ley lines illustrate that the planet has evolved in a way that is very geometric, and this has occurred over a great number of years. Yes, one could argue things have been manipulated in that fashion, but there is no proof of this. Nor is there proof of it happening naturally either, so decide for yourself what you want to believe. I prefer the evolution perspective because it is the answer that is most logical to me, but choose what works best for you.

These vortices exist around the planet, and they are the energetic foundation for the sacred sites that were discussed above. Usually, sacred sites were built on vortices, and it was almost done in a way that seems almost subconscious. For example, some could say that ancient people instinctively knew where these vortices are. However, it could be just as fair to say that they were guided to these vortices by some prater-human intelligence or source. We'll never know, but we can speculate through the power of belief. The fact of the matter is that ancient people built sacred sites on vortices, and on a side note, a lot of times the bigger the vortex, the more prominent the sacred site.

However, as many as are known, many, many more remain unknown and only exist in local lore and legend across the globe. There are a few common traits to know in order to learn how to spot them for yourself. The first trait is that there will always be something "outstanding" about the location. This can be something as simple as things growing better there, or more complex, such as people that spend a lot of time there are extra fortunate in life in general. There's no firm, hard list when it comes to these traits, so learning them is an ongoing process. The second trait to look for is its significance in local lore, as hinted at above. Usually, at least the location itself plays a defining role in the development of the surrounding civilizations, and another general rule of thumb is that they will still be at work to this day. Oftentimes this also applies to the paranormal and the occult, also known as the supernatural. For those that have developed their energetic skills, you may find you can simply tune in to vortices and sites in your immediate vicinity. But what if you sense a vortex, but when you get there, there are none of the characteristics present that are mentioned above?

These guide the conversation to the concept that not all sacred sites are active, but rather there are some that are dormant. Not all vortices are always active or "on," as it were. Vortices are where ley lines cross, but even the ley line patterns change over time. After all, energy follows the path of least resistance when it comes to how it moves through the multiverse, and there are biological changes that occur to the planet from time to time, which will affect the ley lines and vortices. This means that there are two kinds of vortices, and then by extension, sacred sites: active and dormant. Sometimes vortices become dormant because the flow of energy shifted, as we mentioned above, but sometimes vortices become dormant because they have been depleted or corrupted. Let's look at a hypothetical situation to illustrate the various ways vortices can become dormant.

Let's say someone discovers a vortex and builds a sacred site there. This person was guided to the spot by intuition, energetic sensitivity, the gods, or some other non-physical intelligence. When they discover this spot, they build a temple. This temple stands for one thousand years, with hundreds of people attending it during a year. This number may seem small, but I am downplaying it to keep with the historical feel of the illustration. Then, over time, people quit coming to the temple for various reasons. The people with the gift in the area cannot pick up the same energy they could before. So, tales are made, such as the temple lost the favor of the god, or simply that the energy is gone, and thus the temple should move, too, or simply close its doors. Whatever the story is, the temple goes by the wayside. This is a perfect example of a vortex shifting. Let's say the same temple didn't lose energy over time, but rather a tragic, violent and intense event occurred, so violent that it left an energetic mark on the landscape. This is an example of something happening at the vortex to taint the energy, and perhaps even to deplete it. This would still produce the same effect of the temple no longer feeling sacred, but would be due to a cause perpetrated by the people that frequented there. It then becomes obvious that there are a number of ways to look at this, even, due to the fact that some of the people that perpetrated the violent and intense events may have been corrupted by the energy of the vortex itself due to their subconscious energy sensitivity. In any event, the vortex becomes dormant and/or tainted.

While the dormancy occurs at one vortex, this also means that another vortex is created at a different location. Let's think of this for a moment. If the previous temple goes dormant, then the energy along the ley lines will follow the path of least resistance around the dead zone, and will collect at another new vortex. Logically, then, it may take a while to be there before someone recognizes it, but when it is recognized, a new sacred site may be built on it. Or perhaps someone recognizes the value of what they have, and they hide it from others to keep it to themselves. What was once a vortex for a temple may now be a sacred grove or pool instead, with the owner of the land making sure it stays hidden and protected. When you piece it together, you quickly realize that generally if a vortex moves, it doesn't move that far away, but then again, that idea of "not far away" is highly subjective. It may shift close by, or move a distance of one thousand miles. There are no hard and fast rules for this, but rather broad concepts to tailor as you see fit. Time heals all wounds, and the original vortex may come back to its original spot, however many millions of years it may take. In the case of major, geological influences, ley lines may shift, so that particular vortex may never reform. There are almost endless numbers of ways this could play out, and the only limit is your imagination and creativity.

Not all vortices are created equally though, and this tells us they can be of varying strength. You may have a strong vortex in one place, and a minor vortex in another, and there may be various reasons for this. However, a good rule of thumb is that around every major vortex there are usually several minor ones, in some sort of rough pattern. Generally there are three strengths of vortices: weak, intermediate, and strong. Of course these are my guidelines and are quite vague, but they do serve as a rough estimate to work with as we refine our wisdom in that area. Sometimes you may have a large vortex surrounded by two or three medium strength vortices, or half a dozen small vortices.

There is an interesting tangent along these lines though, and that is that as a species we can *create* vortices! This can be done through psychic energy manipulation methods and techniques over an extended period of time. To illustrate, think of a temple that is nowhere near a vortex, but it is so popular that many, many people attend it over an extended period of time, and the energy behind their beliefs accumulates over time, pooling together and forming a vortex. You could apply this line of thought to the damaged vortices mentioned above as well. The general rule of thumb when it comes to creating a vortex is that the more psychically talented someone is, the more energy they have access to, and the more they can affect their surroundings in this way. And, of course, the same rule of energy applies here: the more people that are gathered together to do energy work, the better, and the energy present will be exponentially increased, which helps to make the vortex faster and stronger. However, the tradeoff is that if people stop building energy there, it will dissipate and fade over time.

Ley Line Details

Now let us turn our attention to some details that generally get glossed over when it comes to discussing ley lines, energy, sacred sites, or vortices. Let's discuss some finer points. One of the first that comes to mind is that energy can be more easily sent via ley lines than not. What this means in a traditional sense is that if you live and do magical work near a ley line, your energy and intent is being propelled via that ley line, which magnifies it and expedites its manifestation process. This also means that non-physical beings can travel these ley lines, and the best illustration to define this is to think of it as the difference between driving on a two lane country road versus taking the interstate to your destination. Theoretically, communication can travel these lines as well, and the entire ley line may share an identifying characteristic that can be spotted in a different geographical location. From a continental perspective, ley lines may be connections for powerful vortices. The clearest example of this I can think of is that it is said that the Cahokia civilization in North America, located east of the Mississippi river, but near modern day St Louis, lines up via ley line with Chaco Canyon, located in the state of New Mexico in the United States of America. These two civilizations are thousands of miles apart, so while trade between them was definitely possible, it is not known whether or not it was likely or even occurred. However, both of those civilizations left an indelible mark on the history of Native Americans and the history that has occurred since they were at their heights centuries ago. Could the natives simply have tuned into the energy present without any knowledge of the others' existence? Who knows?

Another detail to know is that if you live on a ley line, or near one, you're going to have a more active life than someone that doesn't live near one, and if you're born near one, it will impact you for the rest of your life. Let's define what near one is, though. In astrolocality, a branch of astrology, a person's birth chart is laid on the globe to see strong and challenging places, and when studying it, there is an orb of influence of 750 miles in any direction. The orb of influence for a vortex or a ley line would be very wide indeed, but a hard and fast number of miles may not be accurate, as smaller vortices would have smaller orbs of influence than large ones, etc, etc.

Ley lines can just as easily attract creatures to them as well, which means if you are near a ley line, you may get unexpected visitors in large quantities, or at unexpected times. It is easy to see that someone may feel like they are haunted, but in reality they are simply noticing that there is a lot of traffic in the spirit world around them. However, instead of thinking about the environment, they think it is something about them. Thus the takeaway lesson is that when you notice you're in a spiritual high traffic area, it is wise to assess the environment and to put things into context of the environment rather than trying to superimpose some sort of egoic perspective. A very stark illustration of this can be found in the tales of northern and western Europe when it comes to the fey folk, whose stories can be found in many different cultures. For the most part, they are generally considered to congregate in sacred groves or other exotic locations. When you look at those stories through these lenses, you could say they congregate at vortices.

The Four Planes, Ley Lines, and Vortices

I've chosen to focus on the energetic side of ley lines and vortices, thereby skipping a planar breakdown of them because when it comes to applying the planes to these concepts, it doesn't work out too well. The ley lines and vortices are simply energy, and thus they don't necessarily have a preference when it comes to the astral, mental, physical, or spiritual side of things. That's the way raw energy works: It simply exists, neutral in a lot of ways, and any sort of characteristic that applies to it has been placed there by sentient beings for an extended period of time. In short, there's really no such thing as a mental plane vortex or spiritual plane vortex. A vortex is simply a vortex. Later in the next chapter I discuss exceptions to this rule, but for now simply consider ley lines and vortices as being free of the traits of the planes.

The only major point to be aware of that hasn't been discussed yet is whether they are positive or negative. When I use these two terms in this book, I am actually referring to things that are either active or passive in nature, and thus the terms positive and negative are used in the same way as nodes on a battery. Now that we're past the politically correct disclaimer, let us continue. Earlier I defined what they were, but let us take a closer look. You can have positive ley lines or vortices, and you can have negative ley lines or vortices. Really, the best way to think of these terms is that positive equals active, and negative equals passive. So, you can have a vortex that is passive, and one a few hundred miles away that is active. What this means on a day to day level is that you may get very good at sensing active vortices, but may not be as good when it comes to sensing passive vortices, or the converse could just as easily be true. It is rare to find a vortex that is an equal balance of both, but they do exist. This concept of passive and active is true for ley lines as much as for vortices, so you may have ley lines that are receptive to the energy sent their way, or you may have ley lines that have so much of their own energy that they transmute or absorb energy that is sent their way.

In this way, we can see that the ley lines and vortices across the planet form a latticework of energy, very similar to the energetic body of a person that we discussed in previous chapters. Thus they constitute the energetic body of the planet. This fulfils the Hermetic axiom of "as above, so below," and shows the macrocosm to our microcosm. Just like we have etheric doubles, so does the planet, and these spots and features constitute how alive the planet is in various places, all the way to how energetically dead an area is, globally speaking. A good parallel that can be drawn is that the vortices are the chakras of the planet, and thus they usually line up to sacred sites, while the ley lines are the nadis that connect the chakras/sacred sites.

Yes, following this line of logic through then, it would mean that the earth has an astral plane, a mental plane, and a spiritual plane. I will address some of that here and in the next chapter, but for now it is wise to ponder this for deeper pearls of wisdom. The astral body of the planet is what we have been discussing, but let us turn our attention to the mental body of the planet. Take a moment to ponder how that might exist to you. What would it look like? What would it entail? How would it manifest into reality?

Let's look at those bodies of a person to gain further insight into this phenomenon. Let's start with the mental plane. To the human, the mental plane is the plane of logic, order, reason, and all things happening in accordance with order and evolution. However, at the higher levels it is the plane of abstract thought and reason. Thus when you apply that concept to the planet, we can see there are clues around us to ponder. The first one that comes to mind is the commonly found repeating pattern of the wild Fibonacci sequence, and how you discover it in animals and other forms of life all over the globe. The Fibonacci sequence is a series of numbers that is a combination of the ones before it. For those of you that are familiar with the sequence, you can easily see this is a condensed explanation for the sake of brevity. In addition to this numerical sequence, there is also a dimension of this that has to do with particular shapes when you put the numbers on grid paper. This forms shapes, and what is interesting about this is that while it's a human made concept, it also occurs in nature, making it more of a human discovery of something occurring naturally in nature. What I mentioned above is a reference to this numerical sequence occurring in nature. There are specific geometric shapes that can be found all throughout nature, and those could be seen as the mental plane of the planet manifesting into reality. Another way that it manifests lies in the evolution of the physical planet itself. When certain tectonic plates grind against each other to produce an earthquake, for example, we can infer this is the influence of the mental plane because this is what is happening behind the scenes, and the earthquakes are the results. Any time that the planet has brought things into balance through evolution, it has exercised its mental plane onto reality. The best concept I can think of to illustrate this is the fact that nature abhors a vacuum. If a vacuum is created, something will come along and fill it. When it comes to the spiritual plane of the planet, we can only broadly theorize what may reside there. Are there entities that the planet knows about that it would consider its deities? It is already safely assumed that creatures exist that we can't even fathom, and the same could be said for the deities that we are mentioning here. Theosophy takes it so far as to say the planet has a consciousness, and that the lord of the world is Sanat Kumara, but that is another tale for another time. It is entirely plausible and logical to consider the planet having a consciousness, though, and that is something to ponder. A common point of contention among metaphysicians is whether we are separate from that or not, and the debate is going to continue for quite some time. Could we be the deities of the earth? Also, would it be pretentious to think that? It is at this point we arrive at the threshold of belief, so from here subjectivity begins to reign supreme, and beliefs are the dominating factors, so it becomes a theological discussion, which means I'll drawn the line, other than to say that when you're dealing with spirits, first and foremost it is wise to be strong in your beliefs, no matter what they are, for the strength and veracity of your beliefs is what will carry you through your interactions with them to a successful conclusion.

If you know the map, which is what this chapter has been about, then it becomes easy to identify what plane an entity is from, which means that you can identify its strengths and weaknesses, as well as preferences and distastes. This puts you in a position to assess things a lot more analytically, which means you're in a position of greater control of yourself, and thus your personal power is increased. However, knowing the material in this chapter is not enough. There will be plenty of situations that will challenge and possibly even change your beliefs on some things because the map is not the territory, but the psychological structure created by what we have been discussing can provide an excellent and effective beginning point for your reality map.

I'm sure you can read between the lines of what is written up to this point that can help you tweak this model to your own preference and tastes. The concepts I have used up to this point are broad and logical, but they are not the only points to consider. However, it is at this juncture that we move in a different direction and begin to move into spirit contact. While the next chapter still falls in this section of the book, it is the bridge between the self that we have been discussing here, and the actual art of contact itself, which is what the next section of the book will entail. You may want to pause for a few moments after this chapter to draw or write your reality map in your journal. The main reason for this is that once you learn how to interact with spirits and the spirit world in a more proactive way, the more you're probably going to find that your view of reality changes. While this does take openness and courage, it also takes clear mental control of your faculties and discipline over your behavior. It requires intelligence, methodical thinking, and analytical skills to navigate the spirit world safely, and to interact with spirits safely as well.

Yes, you are picking up on that clearly. Interacting with the spirit world and spirits is not always a safe course. There are some spirits out there that some could perceive to be deceptive or dangerous to deal with, and we will discuss those in upcoming chapters. For now, though, simply begin a new section in your journal, or perhaps a whole new journal, that is your progress from this point forward when it comes to interacting with spirits and the spirit world. Let's take my perspective and discard it even, by saying that all spirits are 100 percent on the level and completely made of white light and sunshine. Okay, then the danger still exists that you spend more time in the spirit world than you do in the physical world, and that is almost as unhealthy as you can be. When people spend too much time there, they start to exhibit certain traits. As a hint, I will also tell you that these clues can also be used to determine situations of possession, but that is another story. Oftentimes, when people are spending too much time in the spiritual world, they may lose their bearing in the physical world. You know I'm fond of using examples, so here's another one to illustrate the point. Let's say you know someone that recently had a spiritual awakening. As you watch their life unfold, they become full of puppy energy, and become almost addicted to working with their newfound ability of communicating with spirits and spending time in meditation or astral travel. As you watch, you start to notice that the quality of their life goes down drastically, and they find reasons to spend more and more time meditating or astrally projecting, rather than making sure their physical needs are met and their bills are paid. Eventually, the people in their life turn their backs on them, and the person becomes destitute if they haven't righted themselves yet. Of course this opens the door to a poorer use of their discretion skills, and things spiral downwards from there. Yes, too much of a good thing applies here in full force. Another trait you may notice in those kinds of people can be found in their eyes. Sometimes it's a glazed over look, and other times it's a thousand yard stare, but there's always something telling about the eyes of someone like this. There is a time to work with spirits and a time not to, so developing your discerning and boundary skills with this is of the utmost importance to health and success.

Chapter 5: Astral Phenomena

Thus far we've been speaking of astral beings and some of the scenery you may encounter there, but there is a lot more to the astral world than that. The astral plane is full of many amazing wonders and beauties, and only some of them can be conveyed in this chapter. It is a point of fact that the astral world and what you find there is the threshold to the inner mysteries. These are mysteries that are oftentimes discussed in various occult texts, and yet they are only hinted at rather than outlined in detail because a lot of them are subjective gnostic experiences rather than objective facts to be mulled over. It is for this reason that I cannot, nor will I try, to shed light on all of the astral phenomena that are out there, but rather to share with you some of the ones I've heard about, or have experienced for myself.

The first point to be aware of is that, as mentioned in a previous chapter, your initial point into the spirit world is your astral temple. The beautiful thing about this though, is that its appearance and function can be anything you want it to be, so there are no restrictions when it comes to creating your sanctuary. However, with enough repetitive training, you may start to find that this is where you go subconsciously whenever you are journeying to the astral world. This also means that it is a place you can return to, if necessary. Why would it be necessary, you ask? There are many, many things on the astral plane, but it is not white light, sunshine, and rainbows like people generally think. Rather, the astral can be a place of horrors and unmentionable pain, and sometimes, in order to get away from those places, it is wise to return to your astral temple. There will be those people out there that say something like "But I had an experience and was prevented from returning to it! What now?" Well, quite honestly, when it comes to the astral plane, everything is fluid and in line with your Will, which means that the only thing preventing you from returning to your astral temple is your own perceived weakness. The astral plane is the bridge between objectivity and subjectivity, and is a space that exists in both, so our willpower is our strongest tool while we are there. Thus the idea of being prevented from returning falls by the wayside, shed in the light of inner strength and a strong Will.

There are also two facets to astral phenomena: the manifestations that occur in this physical world we inhabit that are largely ego based, and the situations we find ourselves in when we are astrally traveling. Let's break these down and look at them in greater detail.

Manifestations on the Physical Plane

As we discussed earlier in the book, the astral plane also greatly corresponds to emotions, and at this point we should also keep in mind that the lowest points of the astral plane cross over into the physical world. The reason this is important to keep in mind right now is because our emotions can physically manifest in the physical world. This is oftentimes discussed in metaphysics in that many points of sickness and disease may take the shape and form of something wrong in the physical body. Thus when it comes to the emotional side of the astral plane, you may find physical manifestations related to health arise, and thus we can use that as a guide to our own personal growth and development. For example, problems with sight usually correspond to not being able to see something clearly in your life. The general rule of thumb, if you're right handed, is that the right side of the body corresponds to the mental plane and all things related to moving forward, whereas the left side of the body corresponds to the emotions and all things related to the past, or at least being stuck in the past. If you're left handed like I am, simply reverse the correspondences. As you can tell, the principle at work behind the scenes is that the dominant hand or side of the body has to do with the mental plane, whereas the weaker corresponds to the emotional plane, and thus in this case the astral plane. There have been many good books written on the subject, so for those of you that are interested in this, you should have plenty of resources to utilize.

This is only one of the ways the astral plane can manifest on the physical world, but let's look at another example. Sometimes it's not that metaphorical, but rather more visceral and immediate. For example, sometimes you can see things from the astral by simply training your clairvoyance as we discussed previously in the section on clairvoyance and then again on astral attachments to the aura. The more your clairvoyance is developed, the more defined these images will be. As this occurs, you may find you see things on a daily basis that give you pause for thought and make you look twice. To the uninitiated, this falls under the excuse of "my eyes are playing tricks on me," but that concept is wrong due to the alchemical imagination we discussed earlier. Thus it should not be considered uncommon to have more and more visions on the physical plane as you develop your psychic skills. Many people are surprised when they began to have those experiences, but it is natural to have these things happen. The key to success though, is to ignore (or better yet, cut out of your life) the people that try to convince you you're delusional, or in some other way mistaken. But, because it's a role I play often (and well, as I've been told), let's play devil's advocate. What if I'm 100 percent off my rocker and that what you're seeing is only a fig newton of your imagination? Well, then enjoy those fig newtons instead of ones that tell you that you can fly, or to perform horrific acts! In either case, the mind believes they are real visions, and thus they are real. Period. End of story.

So thus we see that there are two very distinct and separate ways that the astral plane can manifest in the physical world, and the trick to working with this information is to remember that these are not mutually exclusive ideas, but rather they can overlap. For example, if you start seeing things from the astral plane on the physical plane, and they are disturbing things, then it would be wise to pay extra attention to your health and the correspondences we mentioned above having to do with dis-ease and dis-comfort manifesting. Doesn't this make the astral plane more tangible? Isn't it interesting how the physical and astral planes overlap? This is the kind of thinking to embrace and work with when you are looking at the four planes as states of consciousness in addition to dimensions, if you will.

Speaking of dimensions, let's discuss those for a moment, since oftentimes the model of the four planes comes into conflict with multi-dimensional writings, and it can seem confusing or almost contradictory when you give them a cursory glance, but they flow together if you look deep enough. The concept of dimensions that is currently kicked around in today's society talks about different dimensions, which are basically big "what ifs." The general idea behind it is that those are alternate states of "reality" that are comprised of situations having played out differently, and thus there are multiple different consequences that are playing out. Another dimensional model that you may encounter is that there are higher dimensions (the 4th, 5th, 11th, etc), and the energies and beings there are of a higher vibration, but do interact with us to assist our growth. And of course by default there are beings on this dimension, the most concentrated, that seek to stop us from evolving. While it does sound like a science fiction model, there is a lot of wisdom in knowing and learning about other dimensions because they help stimulate us to work with the four plane model and increase the work we do with our individualized consciousness. Why do I bring it back to the four plane model? I do because there are countless dimensions, constantly in action and changing, replicating into more dimensions and becoming fractal. This is in play all the time, but you want to know the best part? "A man (person) cannot serve a master in the spiritual world and in the physical plane." (paraphrase of the Judeo-Christian Bible, the book of Matthew, chapter six, verse 24) In other words, it's all about focus. Wherever your attention is, that's where you're at. It's actually karmic law, as I discussed in *Vocal Magick*: "Wherever you go, there you are." Thus all dimensions are infinite and occurring at the same time as this one, so we can tap into them by shifting our attention to them. That is a topic for another time though, but I bring this up now to show how the two models fit together. When you're looking at dimensions, the location on the four planes model depends on the type of dimension. The concept of a physical/visceral plane, astral/emotional plane, mental plane, and spiritual plane, is observed because they are states of being, and thus everything and nothing fits in them, for they are omnipresent. There is one final planar model to look at for the sale of inclusiveness, and that is the four worlds model from the qabala.

According to qabalistic teachings, there are four worlds that the qabala manifests in and through. There are four worlds, and each one emanates out from non-being into being. The highest world, for our purposes, is the world of Atziluth, which is the world of emanations, and is comprised of an entire tree of life within it. This is how the qabalistic worlds are arranged: with one full tree of life in each of the planes. This works very well with the Hermetic axiom of "as above, so below." It also emphasis an important fact that Enochian magic addresses, which is that each "world" (or element) has contained within it the other elements, and their strength and prevalence is determined by elemental (and thus planar) compatibility. The second world, or at least second highest, is the world of Briah, which is the world of creation. As you can see, it's an extension of Atziluth. In Atziluth, we have the first emanations of an idea, but in the world of Briah we start to bring it into focus. The third world is that of Yetzirah, which is formation, which is an extension of Briah. This is where things take shape and form. Finally, in the fourth world of Assiah, we have physical manifestation, or as we know it, the physical world we inhabit. You can see that I am only hitting key points here, but you may also be asking yourself what this has to do with astral phenomena, too. The connection is that you may experience things on the astral plane that are far removed from the physical plane, and by using the reference points of the tree of life and the worlds contained therein, you can psychologically understand what is occurring. When dealing with planes beyond the physical, the most important tool we have is the mind. Another interesting point about the four worlds of the qabala is that you can use those four worlds as a magical thought process, but that is a discussion for a later time.

You see, it is far easier to train the mind to analyze things it experiences than to attempt to make a full and complete list of what can be experienced on the astral plane. Thus before I move into phenomena I am aware of, I wanted to share this information with you so that you are clear on the models you choose to use for yourself as you move forward on your own subjective, personal gnosis/spiritual path. No one person in physical form knows all of the phenomena that exist on the astral plane, so if you read someone saying that or leading you to believe that, run far and fast because they don't know. They may have ideas, philosophies, and concepts from their path that are useful, but they are not the "be all end all" source on the astral plane. No one in form is, because all beings that are in physical forms have a flaw, if not more. What we're discussing here is magical thinking, or viewing what you experience through a magical lens rather than a normal consciousness one. But that is a conversation for another time. Let us move on to the second point.

Astral Plane Manifestations

For further clarification, I am going to break this down into two further categories: environmental and creatures. The reason for this should be obvious.

Environmental Manifestations

The first point to be aware of is that the regular laws of physics don't apply here, and thus anything is possible. This opens the door to a realm of possibility that is limitless, but there is one pervading theme, which is that of desires and emotions. While the laws of physics don't come into play, what's in your heart, does. This also addresses attachments, both healthy and not, and in a lot of ways can be seen as our passions and desires played out unfurled and unfettered.

Because of this, you may witness and experience many, many different things when you astrally travel in whatever capacity. You may witness beautiful rainbows and waterfalls, as well as objects floating where they shouldn't be due to a lack of gravity. Or, you may experience all of your passions and desires coming true. Hence the scenery may vary from emotion to emotion, which is why it is wise to maintain mental control and calm. One of the keys to successfully navigating this realm is to remember that what you're seeing is the environment of the personality self and not the ascended self, which I will write about in future volumes. In other words, you're experiencing the "every human" sensations, and what we experience while we're here in physical form.

However, you may also experience environments that you don't think ~could~ exist, or ones that are perversions of what you may know. This is a certain sort of trickiness that we will discuss in the next section of the book, but for now it is enough to note that it exists. You may see the sites of the planet Mars, for example, but romanticized as your imagination makes it. Yes, that means that time doesn't exist here, so you can visit and experience Atlantis and ancient Egypt as much as futuristic Tokyo. This is something that has been written about extensively in other places, so I won't go in depth with it here. It is just enough to know that time doesn't exist, and thus you can work with the astral plane as much as the physical plane. However, because the astral plane is the plane of desire, some people get addicted to it, and choose to spend more time here than they do in the physical plane. That is one of the dangers that goes with this place: addiction. I have known many people through my life that spend more time on the astral than the physical, and this leads to a decrease in the quality of life on the physical plane. Loosely this is called living in spiritual fantasy rather than spiritual reality, and it is a danger to be avoided. It is far easier to live in an astral world of our creation than it is to pay the bills and be stable in the physical world. Yet we're here to work through physical and societal karma, so it's counterproductive to engage in spiritual fantasy. That just seems silly to do!

However, since the astral plane is a shifting landscape largely based on desires, this also means that it can shift at a moment's notice. Hence, if your emotions or moods change, then so does the landscape. As an example, you may find that on the astral you're walking along a country road on a bright sunny day, but if your thoughts stray to darker ideas, then you may find yourself walking along a lonely country road at night, with a storm on the horizon. For the inexperienced astral traveler, this may be particularly disconcerting. Of course the irony is that it was brought on by the individual, but I digress. The obvious way to avoid this is to be in control of your emotions when you astral travel. The good news is that with a shift of consciousness you can change your environment, too. If you find yourself in a particularly nerve-wracking environment on the astral, you can shift your scenery to a better place, and this trick to success for this lies in knowing the place that you are envisioning, rather than believing it exists. You see, that's one of the esoteric things you learn when you walk this path, and that is that there is a difference between knowing the path and believing the path. Yes, for those of you that are fans of the movie *The Matrix*, that is where this concept comes from. Anyone can believe anything, but until they put the whole of their being into living it, it's still just a belief. When you walk the path, you come to realize that there is a place beyond belief, and that is the place of knowing. However, for each person this is a different paradigm. The one thing I can tell you for sure is that you'll always know who knows it because there will be something about them in their eyes. You may not be able to identify it, but you will simply know it. For some, it's a haze that is in their eyes, but for others it is a certain spark that you see with your mind's eye. Those are the ones that know their path rather than simply believing it. They are usually gentle souls, though, because they're focused on what they're doing and in sharing that with the world, so petty notions generally don't affect these people in many ways. It's almost like they have one foot in the physical world and one in the astral world, and it makes them seem otherworldly. Some of them are conscious of this, and others are not, so you always want to exercise discernment and respect in conversations. However, then again, isn't that the way you want to interact with everyone, anyway? I mean, if you're approaching life from a space of love...

Thus, when traveling the astral plane, be aware of your control, and remember how to address your consciousness as we've discussed above. Now let us turn our attention to the creatures you may find there, and how they may manifest.

Creature Manifestations

I think you'll see that the same line of thought is present here, and that is that anything can happen and/or be experienced. When it comes to creatures you may encounter in the astral plane, it's safe to say that you may encounter anything and everything here. Demons, angels, gods, and all creatures in between can be found here, and because of this, an open mind is an important asset to have. However, one rule of thumb is that the only creatures that are generally found here are those that are already in your subconscious and/or your imagination. If it's not part of your spiritual paradigm, you are probably not going to encounter it. This is good news indeed, because what it means that the more you control what you're exposed to in the physical world, the more you are in control of what you see and experience in the astral world. There are a few exceptions to this, though, that we'll discuss below.

What makes this space interesting is the fact that sometimes you may encounter creatures you don't recognize. Does that seem contradictory to you? It seems contradictory to me, but let's explore it a bit more in depth. These creatures may take the shape of creatures that you've never seen, yet are tied to you because they may be your fears made flesh as it were, and thus while you may not recognize them, they may still represent something that is emotionally important to you. For example, if you have a fear of water, you may find at some point you are confronted with a creature from the depths of the ocean. Psychospiritually you may find it represents something monstrous coming out of your subconscious. However, this is the astral plane, so it is more likely that you are seeing an ancient sea creature rising up to devour you rather than teach you a spiritual lesson. In either case, the point to remember that can assist you is that you are in control of your astral landscape, and thus there is nothing to fear.

There is also the possibility that they are creatures from another time. There have been many creatures throughout the centuries that have gone extinct, but they still remain on the astral plane. Thus it can be common to see a mastodon or a stegosaurus, if they are part of your personal paradigm. However, a caveat to this is that you may discover "fantasy" creatures too, such as dragons, unicorns, and the like. This is because the astral plane is the plane of the imagination, and creatures that have been talked about and worked with over the centuries exist here. This also includes creatures that are part of popular culture, and characters from popular culture, too. In short, the more dynamic the creature you encounter, the more they are believed to be real on the physical world. Let's look at the Star Wars phenomenon. As many millions of people have loved the saga over the last few decades, there has been a lot of energy built up in those concepts, and thus on the astral plane the characters and animals do exist. All of this has to do with thought forms and egregores, and because of this, it is wise to pay attention to what is out in society, but it is also wise to pay attention to where your energy and attention goes as well, for you are feeding certain concepts that exist on the astral plane with your energy.

One final note to keep in mind as we move into the next chapter and section of the book is to remember what was discussed earlier about each plane having seven subplanes. This is important because it reminds us that there are lower planes to the astral world, and there are higher planes. Therefore, if we find ourselves surrounded by things that seem scary or dark, we can change to higher subplanes without leaving the astral. Of course it is also good to leave the astral, but I reiterate this here because sometimes it is easier for us to rise to a new subplane than it is to rise to a whole new plane. In other words, it's like going from zero miles an hour to thirty miles an hour, then to sixty miles an hour, rather than going from zero to sixty straight away. What this means on a practical level is that we can move in increments in the non-physical world, rather than feeling like we have to make absolute choices and extreme movements. This becomes a very profound teaching when we see how this thought process can help us in manifested life. Physical incarnation is a sliding scale of grey rather than a world of absolutes, and because of this, the more we work with this sliding scale in physical form, the better we prepare ourselves for non-physical adventures. By putting principles like this into practice now, we put ourselves in a better position to deal with the non-physical later in this life and in the spirit world.

The reason this is important to keep in mind is that when we are contacting spirits of any variety, we may accidentally or unintentionally fall into an absolutist mindset, and generally this is counterproductive to communication. If we snubbed our nose at every spirit that came along, we would be sending the message that we are only interested in superficial appearances, which is quite shallow of us. A common teaching of magic and metaphysics is that sometimes higher vibrational beings will choose visages that are not at all what we expect, so if we base spirits solely on their appearances, we are choosing not to dive deeper via critical thinking, which short circuits our growth. Yes, we can sense the vibration of spirit beings with our own senses, but that means that we have refined our skill over those senses to be better than our five physical senses. A perfect example of this is seeing a skeleton in the spirit world. Due to programming from society, we may turn a blind eye to it almost instinctually, but what if that spirit is the spirit of a human from a long time ago that is getting our attention so that we can help it move on to the next stage of its existence? To me, that's a gamble that is unwise to take. If we can adjust our consciousness to looking beyond what our sight shows us, we can make great strides forward in our efforts to interact with spirits and the spirit world.

We now come to the close of part two of this book, and this is also the completion of the background information I feel is necessary to work with spirits and the spirit world in an effective and educated manner. From here on out the book will be focused on techniques and methods for spirit contact. However, the techniques that are listed in these first two sections are techniques that you can come back to time and again to hone your skills, and to share with others so they improve theirs. I'm sure that many of you are reading this material and thinking to yourselves that it may contradict what you have learned through your spiritual paradigm, and when those moments occur, take from this text what is applicable and leave the rest. I do my best to counteract dogma whenever possible, so when in doubt, default to your personal belief system, since it is the one that you have an emotional and spiritual connection with. That will trump what I or anyone else outside of your spiritual paradigm says every time. The information I share here is meant as an enhancement and clarification of things that are not often discussed in the occult, and thus it is supplemental to your own personal development path.

Part Three: Spirit Contact

Chapter 6: Channeling and Mediumship

So much has been written on this chapter, yet the more I read and am exposed to, I see that not enough has been written on it. There are two words that you will often see used in conjunction with spirit work, and those are "channel" and "medium." Yes, this also includes all derivatives of the words, which include "channeling" and "mediumship," to name a few. According to the *Oxford English Dictionary*, channeling "serve[s] as a medium for" something, usually spirits. Also, according to the Oxford dictionary, medium means "A person **claiming** to be in contact with the spirits of the dead and to communicate between the dead and the living."

To clarify, the body is the channel, and the medium is the person. Another alternative definition of the word medium has to do with art and creativity. For example, the *medium* on which something is created, is the most commonly understood concept, as in an artist using charcoal pencils as the medium to convey their art. While the terms are used interchangeably, there are those very detailed differences to know. In this chapter we are going to look at both concepts in the name of clarity. This is a fine detail that I have found all too lacking in a lot of books on mediumship and channeling. These concepts are not interchangeable, yet oftentimes they are used that way. We will look at both as separate concepts, which will also reveal overlap in a lot of ways, and we will look at how to work with both.

However, as much as I'm separating them, I'm also showing *how* they work together, for ninety-nine percent of the time they are used in tandem with one another, so to only study one concept or the other would be remiss, and to only study them together is equally bad. Critical thinking tells us we should look at them individually and together. It is simply wise to delineate concepts in the name of clarity, and therefore it makes sense to start here.

Channeling

Let's start off with what channeling is, and what it isn't. Contrary to popular belief, you can be good at channeling but not at mediumship. But, how, Bill? I've never read that before! What do you mean? Well, let me break it down. The easiest way to understand it is to think of a channel that water runs through, something like a man-made river or gulley. A channel is what something travels through, and in our text we are referring to the person, but as you can see from above, channeling a consciousness is very parallel to water traveling through a channel. Hence, someone can be very good at putting their consciousness aside. Water is an excellent metaphor for energy that has been used for a very long time, and it holds true in this case as in every other. With what we're discussing here, it makes things clearer if we keep this in mind through this last section of the book. For our practical purposes, let's work with the image that the human body is the channel. That means that there are physical limits to what we can channel. Yes, this can be worked with and modified to a large degree, but this still holds true in a lot of ways. The reason for this is that we are in a physical existence, and because of this, we adhere to physical laws, which means we have physical limits. We can no more grow an arm out of our forehead than we can fly.

When first beginning to channel, this is wise to keep in mind because it also provides a framework to work within. If we are mindful of this, we can focus on the development of our skills and not get dragged into spiritual fantasy. The lesson we take away from this is to focus on our physical health first and foremost to the best of our abilities. This is our due diligence and daily maintenance of our channel. The more we physically deteriorate, the more we negatively impact our ability to channel. Yes, there is an exception or two to this, but by and large, this is simply true. For example, the spirit of an athletic swimmer wouldn't necessarily be at home or comfortable in the body of an overweight, old and sick armchair magician, unless there was another mitigating factor, like the channel reminding him of a parent. Succinctly, perspective and context are two major themes to be mindful of when preparing the channel.

There are two facets to this to note, so let's take a moment to address them here. The first facet is addressing this on an ongoing basis. Diet, exercise, regular doctor visits, and all things related should not be neglected in the name of spirit contact. All of those should be regularly performed to the best of the abilities of the channel. I'm not going to assume that this is the same for everyone though, so use your best judgment as to how to address this, but simply know that if you let your body go, you're inhibiting your ability for spirit contact to a large degree. An esoteric reason for this is that if you're in poor health when it comes to your legs, then you may not be able to recognize if a spirit has an issue with legs, and thus you're missing an association of the spirit for future reference. Diet is the biggest point to consider when channeling because, as has been said many times before, "garbage in equals garbage out." If you are not mindful of what you put into your body, you're sending the message to the universe that you really don't care what you take in, so the type of energy you'll get from the universe is the same level of beings. This doesn't mean that every meal should be a steak dinner, but rather this refers to grocery lists, supplements, and basically anything that is good for you to take in so that you attract a higher quality of being.

The second facet to note is that of the preparation of the self before a channeling session. A general rule of thumb in occultism is that you want to avoid eating, specifically eating heavy foods, three hours before the spirit contact. When I was first working with this and learning it, I just took it at face value and accepted it because it seemed reasonable, but as I learned, there are actual biological reasons for this. The most obvious is that you don't want to be in the middle of a spirit contact session and have a flatulence attack! That is rude in many different ways, and if it can be avoided, then it should be. One of the best ways to avoid it is to be mindful of what you eat and when you eat it. Something else that I read about the way the human body processes food is that it takes approximately three hours to truly process a meal. Hence, the further away you are from your last meal before channeling, the better off you are. I realize, though, that life happens, and sometimes this is not an option. If you find yourself in this situation, then adapt to the circumstances. Foods that are considered good to eat in a pinch like that includes fruit and yogurt specifically, but can also include any kind of food that is light like those are. Metaphysically, these foods keep the vibration high, and sweeten the body, so to speak. If neither of these are options, then a granola bar or energy bar can work just as well, but only one or two. Theoretically, it will only take one or two to get you through the spirit contact session anyway, and after the session, it is wise to eat foods that ground you and bring you back into your waking consciousness and physical body. Two of the best foods to eat in this instance are meats and grains.

While we have been discussing foods up to this point, let us turn our attention to liquids. There are a lot of adamant perspectives on this out in the world, and I would like to shed some light and perspective on things. To begin with, water is the best liquid to drink to prepare yourself for spirit contact. We are approximately seventy percent water, and because of this, when it comes to hydration, we should make sure we are up on our water intake. Soda is something to avoid, as are related drinks. One of the best drinks you can drink ahead of time is water with lemon in it. While the three hour fast rule doesn't play a huge role in this, it is wise to keep in mind how long it takes water to travel through the body so as to avoid any uncomfortable situations. There is an esoteric reason for this as well, though, and that is that if we are mindful of what we take in when it comes to food and drink, and we keep ourselves as pure as possible, it allows us to establish a base to work from when we are channeling. If we go into every channeling session in the same physical state, or as good as we can make it, it then becomes easier to identify subtle sensations that may be associated with the being. For example, if we ate a salad three hours before the channeling session and only drank lemon water, then we are in a better position to recognize subtle associations attached to the being, and more information is always good to have when dealing with spirits. If you ate a salad three hours before the session, yet during the session the people there smelled pork, you would then know that pork is related to the being in some way, and this can provide a clue as to the ethnicity or preferences of the spirit being.

And now, for the infamous and almost expected perspective on mind altering substances. Quite honestly, there is very little I'm going to say about them, so this may be briefer than you would like. However, it will be very clear by the time I am done so that you can make an informed decision for yourself. After all, you're a channel, and I'm a channel, and I think we can agree that there are different strokes for different folks. What works for one channel may not work for another, and that's okay. Here again, like in the section above, use your best judgment when it comes to your channeling development. In today's politically correct culture, the generic answer would be that you should not be on any mind altering substances when channeling. There's also something else to note for consideration, and that is that old time Spiritualists believed that if you even took one drop of alcohol, you were a damaged channel and were not allowed to work with them in their development circles. Yes, they were that strict about it; however, keep in mind that was the late nineteenth century. We don't live in those times. Let's break the perspectives down so we understand them clearly. The first perspective that says no to mind altering substances is saying that for a very good reason. Their reason is that if you're not influenced by any external stimuli, you are in a better position to understand the consciousness, and to study it clearly. I completely understand that point, and agree with it. However, the other camp in existence says that it is okay to use mind altering substances when contacting spirits. Their perspective is simple, too, and that is that mind altering substances shake us out of our day to day waking consciousness to be in a more open and receptive state to the entities coming through. Hence it increases the doors of perceptions and opens them wider than we could otherwise. Frankly, the way I see it, both sides have good intentions, and both perspectives bring up both points, and like most things in life, the truth is found somewhere in the middle. As the old saying goes, "everything in moderation." Use your own discretion and judgment, but temper it with moderation. I have found that oftentimes it is a sliding scale based on who or what I am contacting. Sometimes mind altering substances can be helpful, but sometimes they are not, and this is also true of sobriety. Sometimes it is helpful, and sometimes it is not. Context tells us that we should be mindful of the culture of the spirit being channeled. If the culture of the spirit being channeled is conducive to mind altering substances, then it is worth considering, but if it's not, then we shouldn't push and force it, either. Another point to think of is that oftentimes you will be channeling when you are around other people, so their perspectives should be taken into account, too. While you may be okay with it, they may not, and this would provide an energetic distraction, so it would be wise to avoid it. Ultimately, just keep your own counsel, but be mindful and respectful of others around you. Moderation should not be neglected though, as many times I've seen people channel while altered, and the quality of being they bring through is much, much lower than they are capable of, so there is something to be said for being sober while channeling.

Now that we've addressed the physical form and how to handle it for highly effective channeling, let us turn our attention inward to the mind and spirit of the channel. While the physical body is the physical plane channel, the heart is the emotional or astral plane channel. If you have a clouded heart, it will greatly impact what you channel. By and large, the way it will affect you is that you will attract beings to you that have to do with emotions and emotional situations that you can empathize and/or sympathize with. This takes us into a slight tangent, so let us ponder that for a second. If what I said is true, and I have seen it true more often than not, then the spirits we contact have messages for us as well as for the others that may be around us when we channel. This is a common rule of thumb, which is that when you bring through messages from a spirit, they more often than not have relevance for you, too. At first this may make you uncomfortable, but with time you can gleam great wisdom from keeping this in mind as you channel. By staying in control of our emotions and approaching life from a position of love, we put ourselves in a position to receive pure and true spirits when we channel. If we are not in firm control of our emotions and our heart, then we limit ourselves to what we can easily channel. Of course this also means it is wise to be emotionally healthy, or at least actively working on that when you begin to channel.

Following heart health comes mental health and knowledge. Let's break it down into those two sections. Let us first look at mental health. To be a truly effective channel, it is wise to be mentally healthy. Some people take this to the extreme and get psychological clean bills of health before engaging in the work on a regular basis. Or you can just make sure you are as mentally healthy as you can get. This also includes more mature concepts as well, and sometimes these trip up good channels. What I'm talking about here are things like discipline, being stable on one's feet, and all things related to living a balanced and productive life. A common phrase that I like to use when assisting people to analyze the results of a channel is to remember the source in all things. I have known many excellent channels over the years that didn't have it together to pay the bills and be stable in the physical world. That is a sign that things are not right within them. I have known many psychics that have lived with elderly parents or in some other way were caretakers for people, and those are the ones that are exempt from this. Look, it's real simple: Someone that doesn't have a firm grasp on the physical world is someone that is going to attract unstable and lower vibrational entities as a general rule of thumb because they are, themselves, unstable. It's simply the law of attraction in action. Does this mean that I think every channel should 100 percent devote their lives to living a channel lifestyle 24/7? No, not at all, for this can be almost as damaging, if not worse. One's best judgment should be used when considering how this will play out in life, but for now it is simply something to ponder. Let's say that you are just opening up to channel, and until now, your life has been largely unstable, so what do you do? Simply put, focus on making sure your life is stable, your responsibilities are honored, and that you are as healthy as you can get. In occult circles this is known as making sure that your house is in order. Esoterically, this is creating a solid foundation to build from to climb to the higher planes. The best rule of thumb to help with this is Maslow's Hierarchy of Needs.

Now let us discuss knowledge, and how important it is. When you are first cultivating your channeling skill, you may find it very useful to expand your knowledge base. This can be learning a new subject, or learning a foreign language, or even simply trying new things. By the way, this should be in addition to learning the subject of channeling. The reason for this is very simple: by increasing your knowledge base, you add another skill to your palette so that you attract more diverse spirits. Spirits will use the most conducive channel to work through, and thus it is wise to continually expand your knowledge base to be a better receptacle for spirits and channeling. This doesn't have to be a lifelong journey, though, as you may simply find one subject that really appeals to you and you dive deeply into it. That is quite all right as well, but keep in mind if you do that, you will attract spirits of that specific type, but they will in a lot of ways be experts of that particular subject above all else. Increasing your knowledge base is how you improve the channel that you are in a more cerebral and thus higher vibrational way. When you expand your horizons, your mind opens up to new possibilities, and because of this, it is easier for spirits to communicate.

Mediumship

Mediumship is something that is quite different than channeling, so let us turn our attention to it for a few moments. If the body, heart, and mind are the pieces of the channel, then what exactly is mediumship? Well, you know the answer to this; you just don't know that you know it. The medium is the actual personality self, so in this way we come to realize that being a medium means having the ability to communicate with spirits, particularly dead ones. Thus we can deduce from the first section of this book, a medium is someone that has developed their psychic skills to the degree that they can interact clearly and competently with non-physical beings of many different types. You may be a wonderful medium, but have a sub-par channel, which happens many times. A way to work through this is to compensate whenever possible through the stimulation of the imagination in addition to the cultivation of the logical, responsible, other hemisphere of the brain. In other words, use both hemispheres of the brain as is appropriate to your work. Our consciousness and developed psychic skills are what make us mediums. Hence the more we develop our psychic skills, the more we can become a better medium. In other words, when we find repeatable results on a regular basis, we should not rest on our laurels and leave our skills stagnant, but rather we should perform basic upkeep on them, keeping them sharp and actively working with them. In a lot of cases, this is actually too easy to do, and we may fall into living in spiritual fantasy land, losing control on the physical plane, so that warning should be remembered here as we discuss keeping your skills sharp. They should not be worked with to the degree they are counterproductive to life! Being a medium means that there is a natural affinity to the spirit world, and that is something that cannot be measured by the channel. That is how they are two separate ideas. To continue our image from above, the channel is the riverbank, but being a medium is the river itself. Understanding that consciousness can flow a lot like water can carry someone forward quickly when it comes to developing their mediumship skills. Keeping this in mind makes it easier to control your shift of consciousness and focus to sense and interact with an incoming consciousness. This metaphor also makes it easy to let go of the reins to allow a mind to come in, yet it should also remind us that we can wash it away just as quickly.

Due to the influence of popular culture and the mass media, certain fantastic ideas have been cast into the mass consciousness of the public, and there are many preconceived notions about channeling, mediumship, and, you guessed it, possession. It seems to me this is the perfect time to enter into these trepid waters, because they are horrifying to look at from the outside, but once you take a closer look through a trained and clear lens, you teach yourself to sniff out the truth from the fiction, not just in the media and popular culture, but also when it comes to the beings themselves. Let's begin with possession. In short, the concept behind a possession is that another consciousness completely takes over the physical body and mind of the medium, thus making them a puppet. Can that happen? Yes, it can. Does it happen often? No, it most certainly does not! What if I don't believe in possessions? Excellent answer, and let me elaborate. You see, true cases of possession usually have to do with particular belief systems and what the followers of that religion believe, rather than an all across the board rule of thumb. The majority of mediums I know do not believe in full blown possessions unless there are other factors involved, which is what I will turn my attention to next. However, I have seen possessions in person many times, and they all share the same characteristic: they are a part of the belief system of the medium. That's interesting to consider, isn't it? Allow me to explain. A full blown possession can be found in the Afro-Caribbean belief systems in many different ways. A full blown possession can be found in all of the Abrahamic faiths and their belief systems. A full blown possession can NOT be found in Thelema. A full blown possession can NOT be found in Spiritualism, to my knowledge, but I am more than open to correction. I think my point is clear. If becoming possessed is part of your belief system, then yes, you can be possessed unless you willfully and intentionally train yourself otherwise. The reason the idea of full blown possession doesn't exist in other belief systems is because in those systems, the strength of will of the individual is emphasized. In short, there is no possession possible because one can simply kick the other consciousness out, because each one of us is divine and has autonomy. I have found this method to work routinely, but admittedly, at first I really struggled with this, too. In time though, the way I worked through it was simply taking to heart our inherent divinity and putting it to work for me, so it was a shift in my consciousness. Hence take this time to ponder what the role of possession is in your belief system before proceeding.

Do you have it sorted? Good. The exercises I gave earlier in this book can be referred to and modified time and again, so feel free to exercise your creativity. The only thing to keep in mind is what your goal is for the modification. Above we discussed possession, so let us shift to other stereotypes that we've been exposed to through various outlets of society. The first one that comes to mind is when the eyes roll back in the head. Um, this generally doesn't happen. I say generally because I have seen it happen once or twice in my life, but when put into context of almost thirty years of experience, I would call that rare, indeed. That is embellishment on the part of entertainers to let us know a shift of some kind is happening. Another embellishment that comes to mind is when a medium contorts in some way. This generally doesn't happen either, but I can think of a handful of cases when this has occurred, so it happens more than many people realize. If you ever find yourself in or around that situation, it's serious. Joking aside, that is usually a sign of something, and as a general rule of thumb, bad, happening. I have been present in one or two, so I can tell you from first-hand experience that it is intense, and those events are what separate the confident medium from the unconfident one. The confident medium will stand steadfast in the confidence of their skills, and will see it through to its conclusion, whereas the unconfident one will get scared and not be able to finish things.

Another stereotype that has only recently begun to change, is that of the appearance of a medium. When I was first learning occultism, the stereotype of what a medium looked like was an old, eccentric, sweet, lady. By the way, there is some truth in that, because that stereotype is based on a real person. However, I digress. So as I learned more and more about occultism, that was the stereotype that was continually driven home to me, and even to this day, in a lot of TV shows or movies from Hollywood, that is exploited and used to a very large degree. It has only been since the explosion of social media and the global community that we have begun to get exposed to enough mediums out there to counter this stereotype. One thing that is all over the internet is that mediums look like everyone else. True, there are those that are eccentric, but by and large that image is fading, and I am enjoying watching it leave! Good riddance! The more people that embrace their psychic skills and even go into being a medium, the more the outdated stereotype is challenged.

Once we get past the stereotypes and the misconceptions, we can move to the real meat of mediumship: the person. I've said it before and I'll say it again. Being a good medium does not equate with being more moral than the average person! In a lot of ways, being a medium automatically makes life more interesting because what the medium can channel through them (see how that works together?) is solely based on their inherent vibration. As an occult example of this, I would like to share the story of Dr. John Dee and Sir Edward Kelly. These were two magicians in the Renaissance that brought information through and gave us the Enochian system of magic. While there is a lot more that can be said about them, I'm keeping it short here for the sake of brevity. What's worth noting is that the character of Kelly was known to be dubious, and the spirits knew this, so when they brought information through, it was coded, and Dr. Dee, who happened to be a cryptographer, had to decode it. This occurred because the spirits didn't trust Kelly, but wanted Dee to have the information. Hence, the shady character of Kelly negatively impacted the information being transmitted. To me, this is the biggest motivator to be on the moral up and up. After all, if you can make average choices in life for the better, and be able to contact better quality of spirits, then why wouldn't you? To me it's just logic.

Yes, this does mean that character improvement is something it would be wise to emphasize throughout the course of your mediumship development. By continually working to better ourselves, we improve the quality of material we'll get from spirits. What it takes to accomplish this is discipline, devotion, and focus, and these are the very reasons why it may be a challenge to do mediumship work 100 percent of the time. It really doesn't allow for a lot of other life areas that some may enjoy. There have been many nights in my life I chose to stay home and work rather than socialize because I had mediumship style work to do. That's a sacrifice that may not work for a lot of people, and I completely understand and support that. Each person has their own dharma, and because of this, each path is different. This is a fine point to keep in mind at the beginning of your mediumship development though, because it assists you in setting up a regimen and routine to follow to cultivate your skill.

So let's turn our attention to said structure, since we addressed diet and the body earlier. Being a medium means that you have cultivated your psychic skills to the degree that you can interact with the spirit world and the spirits that reside there. However, there are also those out there that are naturally born psychics. Oftentimes, this is hereditary, specifically on the maternal side of the family tree, and occasionally it skips a generation. Yes, it can happen spontaneously, but that is very rare. Either way, you have the ability to interact with them. After you realize what psychic gifts you have, and at what strength and competency, you can take your training to the next level and work on producing reproducible results. This is where the trick comes in, and this is also why discipline and a good routine are so important. You can either get carried away in your newfound abilities, getting lost in a honeymoon sort of situation, or you can progress too fast, burning yourself out. Like any other skills, your psychic skills need to be kept up, but they should also be kept in check. The most effective way I've found to address it is to set aside one night a week that you focus on your psychic skills and mediumship. During this night, treat it like a spirit contact session like I mentioned above. Eat light food approximately three hours beforehand, make sure you are hydrated, and are in a place where you will not be disturbed.

As far as clothes are concerned, lighter colors are preferred, especially ones that are loose. Lighter colors are considered higher vibrational, so as you don them, you send the message to the universe that you are consciously raising your vibration in order to attract high vibrational spirits. A subtle variation on that is to wear clothes that correspond to the colors of the spirit you are contacting. Basic color correspondences can be used here, but when in doubt, go with white.

Mediumship Template

Once the above criteria are met, let's discuss the setup. The general rule of thumb is that you want low level light, and the room itself to be on the smaller end of the scale. Traditionally, an oil lamp is preferable, but you can also use votive candles or tea lights. Have at your disposal your journal and pen. If you enjoy incense, then pick one that corresponds to meditation, but since it is a small room, you may want to use Japanese incense with light smoke. Create your sacred space in line with your spiritual path. Once the space has been established, use your preferred developed psychic sense to communicate with the consciousness of another foreign being. This is generally the hardest part because it does take a while to fine tune your psychic antenna, but with practice and experience you will find you settle into it quite nicely. For example, some people will smell a certain scent when a spirit is around. Others may have their hair stand up on end on their arm or down their spine. There are many different tells out there, so feel free to refine it to the degree you're comfortable with, and once you have established that, move on to actually interacting with this consciousness.

The next step is to establish a way to communicate with it. This can be almost anything from hand gestures you see from it extended to you, to arcane symbols that need further research. There are a few things to keep in mind at this point. The first one is that if spirits have a preference, they will connect with you through symbols rather than words. To slow their vibration down to the degree that they can execute speech generally means it's a lower vibrational spirit. The medium should have a broad understanding and knowledge of symbols by this time, and thus they can receive more information than if a spirit slowed down their vibration to the point of speech. Scientifically this should be clear as to why, but if it is not, allow me to explain. If something is vibrating at a high level, it is moving faster, and any sound it generates that we can detect has a higher pitch. Oftentimes we can't even detect that, as in the case of a dog whistle. However, things that are vibrating at a lower pitch tend to produce deep, resonant sounds, and ones that move slower, too. Hence you begin to communicate with it via symbols. How the communication happens is highly subjective and open to adjustment, so feel confident if you make certain changes in line with your belief system. What you're creating at this point is your own basic spirit contact template that you can modify as you grow and evolve.

This step could also include choosing what device you would like to use to see the spirit in, if you have decided to scry it. Almost anything with a reflective surface would work, but there is one caveat I would like to add here for clarification. Do NOT use an Ouija©! The reason for this is that it will attract much lower entities than are safe or worthwhile working with. Part of the answer to this lies in the very board itself. All that is on the board are yes/no questions, the numbers 0-9, and letters of the alphabet, and remember what I said earlier about a spirit slowing itself down to use speech and letters! There are other psychic development boards out there, and some of those are worth considering. As a general rule of thumb, a good psychic development board is one that uses a lot of symbols, specifically more than letters, for starters. It is also wise to avoid pendulums, too, and the reason for that is that pendulums bring information up from your subconscious, so they are not making contact with external beings, but rather they are helping you refine your relationship with yourself. It may seem like this contradicts clairaudience where a person gets a message through sounds, so allow me to clarify. All of the clairs are extensions of the physical senses (and then some, but let's focus on this point for right now), and therefore they are as limited as the five senses. What they focus on is receiving messages from a non-physical source, so yes, each one is limited to its physical counterpart. However, having said that, the clairs that are not extensions of physical senses are a little bit more advanced since they touch into things that cannot be recognized by the five basic senses.

After you've established a way to communicate with it, we move on to the testing phase. This is a step that you may choose not to execute, and that's okay, too. I make it a rule to always test the spirits I work with because there could be imposters, but let's look at the other perspective: karma. Testing your spirits may not be something to concern yourself with for one big reason: the implications. By testing your spirits, you are sending the message to the universe of a lack of self-confidence. In other words, trust is lacking, and if you approach working with spirits from that perspective, you may find your spiritual growth is inhibited in some way. So then, having said that, why do I test my spirits? Quite frankly, I'm a magician. I deal with spirits of all types almost all of the time. I walk the red road, which is the road of grey magic, and thus when I communicate with spirits, they are from all points on the spectrum of vibrations. I don't exclusively deal with one vibration of spirit or another. However, there may be those that are reading this that are mediums and thus are not interested in speaking with the variety of spirits that I do, but rather they want to stay focused on working with high vibrational spirits in general, and that's okay. If this is a step you choose not to address, then skip this section. However, if you decide to test your spirits, this is the point in the template where you would do this. For those of you that think it's a good idea to test your spirits but you don't know where to start, you may want to look into *The Magus* by Francis Barrett, or *The Book of Secret Things, and Doctrine of Spirits*, by Trithemius of Spanheim. *The Magus* contains part of that book, and in both is discussed what to ask spirits and how to verify they are who they say they are. One of the easy rules of thumb to remember is that a higher vibrational spirit will give you a higher vibrational tool or technique to use. For example, a higher vibrational spirit will give you insight into how to deal with pesky relatives, but not tell you where to hide the bodies!

From the testing-the-spirits step until the end of the session, the questions will be audible on your part. So for example, when you ask the spirit a question, ask it out loud, if for no other reason than for those that you are with to hear it. From there, you receive the message from the spirit in a way that is in line with the medium that you are using. For example, if you are gazing into a crystal, you will begin to see an image. If you are using pure clairvoyance, then you will receive a vision in your head. If you are using clairaudience, then you will hear the voice in your head. Oftentimes this occurs hand in hand with clairvoyance, but not always. I have known a few people over the years that could only hear messages, and received no visuals when the message was received. This section of the formula will take the longest, and is the most intense, so I won't put a time limit on this. I also believe it is clear how I am giving you this template, too: flexible enough to take as long as you want at any given step. However, this section is the portion that should last the longest. One of the other points I would like to interject at this point has to do with what to expect when it comes to spirit validation. In various books a particular concept has been used incorrectly and I would like to clear the air. In cases of *true* spirit contact, yes, you will feel a temperature shift in the room, and the room will get warmer, not colder! It is a common misconception that the room will get colder when a spirit is around, but this is not a broad sweeping rule; rather the only time the room gets colder is if you walk through a spirit in a room you may inhabit. When you have a premeditated spirit contact environment, the temperature will rise. Why is this, you may be thinking? Whenever you get multiple people in a small room, laws of thermodynamics tells us that the temperature will rise the more beings that are present, especially ones that emit body heat of some degree. I don't want to tread too far into the realm of ghost hunters here, but I do want to make this very clear. If the room gets colder when you are performing spirit contact, it is because the people present are expending their energy into the room, and thus it feels cold because their core temperature has dropped. Keep this in mind as we move to the next step, which is what to do when you're done.

The next step in the template is what happens when you're done with the communication. The first point to know is that it is wise to thank the spirits for their attendance and answers. Gratitude is one of the best practices to cultivate, and spirits appreciate it as much as humans do. Thus, thank the spirits when the contact is finished, and if applicable, energetically cleanse the physical space to energetic zero, as it were. This is not as important to do if you have a dedicated room for spirit contact, though, so you may find it wise to use your best judgment. Some people say that you don't want to banish in a dedicated space because in that way the energy compounds over the years and experience, so thus spirit contact is easier to achieve and stronger overall. However, some people contend that if you do that, energetic traces are left of the spirits, and thus it can taint the space, so I encourage you to choose for yourself, but whatever you choose, be consistent with it. This doesn't mean you have to decide right now how you will do it for the rest of your life, but rather decide now how you want to proceed, and stay with it. In other words, no lazy decisions on this! If you decide to change your procedure in the future in light of new information, then so be it. That is your free will choice. Also keep in mind that in a true medium session, you will not remember what the entity has said. The basic psychological model that I have found is to think of it this way: While the spirit is in your consciousness, you may feel like a mental fly on the wall observing what it says and will hear the voices of the people that are present that may be interacting with the spirit. However, you work with it, this is important to note. If information is truly channeled, then you won't remember it, but if the information comes from the ego, the medium will remember it, and that's the red flag to be skeptical of them as a medium. The final part of the process is to record these results in your magical journal. The sooner you do this after the session, the better, but do it when you can focus in an uninterrupted fashion to get every detail you can. At this point you may find it wise to see what triggers, guards, and other quirks are part of your spiritual contact procedure, and adjust accordingly.

Chapter 7: Prepared and Spontaneous Mediumship

In the previous chapter we gave an outline of how to conduct a spirit contact event, and while we discussed some things in passing, there are other things that take a few more words to describe, and that is the focus of this chapter. However, I am also going to put a lot of emphasis on a new idea, which is that of spontaneous mediumship. The focus of this chapter is the environment you find yourself in when you are channeling, but since some of this was covered in chapter six, I will put more emphasis on how to handle spontaneous channeling events and environments. This may be of particular use to those that are empaths due to the fact that oftentimes we find ourselves in environments that are outside of our comfort zone and control, yet there is a spirit that is present that wants to make contact with us. While spontaneous mediumship will be a major focus of this chapter, I will also address the environment discussed in chapter six in greater detail.

Prepared Mediumship

This is the kind of mediumship that I used as context for the spirit contact template in chapter six. Prepared mediumship is when you are in the prepared state of mind and in the prepared environment. This is the kind of mediumship that I'm pretty sure most, if not all, would prefer. Largely, this type of mediumship is intent driven, and this is important to note because it means that the medium is going into the environment and situation with a particular desire in mind. This clears the air, pun intended, so that spirits that are conducive to this goal will be congregated around the individual. During the preparation period, no matter how long, spirits will be actively paying attention to the place and event that will be occurring. I say "no matter how long" because if this is a dedicated space for spirit worship, psychic energy will be built up over time, and thus in a very liberal sense, the preparation time has been occurring from the moment you dedicated the space to spirit contact. This means that for experienced workers, the preparation time has been for a number of months or years, and while that preparation time may not specifically be focused on what you are aiming to achieve with this sitting, the effect that has been made has to do with spirits and spirit contact. Hence the whole room becomes more charged with psychic energy, and spirits may gravitate to this location almost unintentionally.

This is also the easiest kind of mediumship to do because of all of the preparation and forward thinking that has been happening for a while, and this means that you are in your own environment. Almost by default, this means that you are in a stronger position, too, since you designed the space and filled it with what you choose. Shortly, I will discuss what should be in it, what shouldn't be, and what is optional, because there are actually quite a few points to be aware of regarding all three topics. A lot of times you find this information piecemeal, which means that it can be hard to go back to, so in this chapter I am going to be as inclusive as I can, and will discuss this in as much detail as I possibly can. Having a dedicated space to do your mediumship work cannot be stressed enough, so I encourage those of you that have the available space to dedicate it to spirit work and to strictly use it at the beginning. There are two major reasons for this. The first one is that it gives you a place to put all the items that have to do with your religious path. The second reason is because it creates mental muscle memory, so that when you enter there, your mind knows you are going to do something special, and shifts consciousness to be more conducive to the work that is done there. Is this a form of self-hypnosis? Why yes, yes it is, and as you develop further in the occult, you will find that a great many things are based on self-hypnosis. When we are executing self-hypnosis, we are basically tricking ourselves into a particular pattern of energy use. It is through these patterns, these rituals that we tap into much more power than we can access with our mental, waking mind. One of the biggest reasons for this is that our subconscious holds most of the power of our mind, and this means that sometimes it's hard to pull that information through. The key point to remember is that self-hypnosis isn't always a bad thing. It's much like manipulation; it gets a bad reputation, but can be just as positive. Anyway, I digress.

Let's discuss what your spirit chamber, as the old time

Spiritualists called it, will look like. Oftentimes it is a room somewhere between 8'x10' and 15'x 6' (or so), but work with what you've got, first and foremost. I've had a lot of rooms dedicated solely to spirit work over the years, and they have been of varying sizes and shapes, so what I mention above are simply guidelines rather than hard and fast rules. Oftentimes I rented a two bedroom apartment and turned one of the bedrooms into my spirit chamber, as an example. There was one time, though, that I simply had a room in the upstairs of a house that had a pointed ceiling, and had odd dimensions to it, so I worked with what I had. The physical part of the environment is sometimes out of our control, so simply be flexible when necessary. Depending on our living situation, we may be "stuck" with a particular room that can be used for spirit contact, and that will dictate how we proceed. This is neither bad nor good because at the end of the day, if it feels right to use and you can justify it, then use whatever space your intuition says.

Once you have your space selected you can begin to decorate it how you see fit. As I'm sure you've guessed, the best way to decorate it is in line with your personal beliefs. All of this is in line with your imagination, so I will spend very little time on it here, other than to remind you to energetically cleanse the room before you begin moving your sacred items in to fill it. After the cleansing has occurred, proceed as your intuition and schedule allows. There are a few rules of thumb to keep in mind, though. The first one is that you want as few electronics in there as possible. This means everything electronic. In short, if you are going to have electronics in there, keep it to an extreme minimum. As an example, a digital voice recorder would be an appropriate sized device. Why, you ask yourself? The more frequencies in the air around the spirit contact chamber, the harder it can make it for the spirit to establish contact. Hence, the smaller the size of the electronic device, the less of an impact it has on spirit contact. An interesting historical question has to do with this, actually. The clarity of information and quantity of channeling has gone down since the founding of Spiritualism in 1848, and some speculate this is because there are more wires in the air and we are using radio frequencies to a very high degree, so it creates a type of static that prevents easy flowing spirit contact. There is some validity to this, though, as sometimes it is easier to do your mediumship work in the middle of a forest or a desert than it is to perform it in a city. I do understand that there are some of you that may want a digital voice recorder to record the event to look for EVP (electronic voice phenomena) when the session is done, and that is usually fine. There is something to be aware of regarding that as well, and that is that oftentimes you cannot catch higher vibrational beings using an electronic device. I experienced this in the late 1990s, and at the time I wasn't active in the community, so I thought it was just an odd situation that I faced. However, when I started meeting more people later, and especially when I did a very brief stint as a ghost hunter, I discovered that this is quite common. Of course the other end of the spectrum is to believe that of course they show up on electronic instruments; that's the whole point of EVP! From my experience, I have seen that a lot of this is based on how high or low the vibration of the spirit is. For a lower vibration spirit, it is easier to be heard on an electronic device, but for higher ones, it is harder to be heard, and generally if the spirit doesn't want to be recorded on there, and they are a very high vibration, then you won't hear them there.

It is always good to decorate the space with bells, chimes, and other things that make noises because this is one of the ways that is easy for spirits to use to contact us. Also of note is that it is wise to decorate your space with flowing items. For example, you may want to use Tibetan door hangings or Tibetan prayer flags. Of course the principle at work here is that if things are hanging, it is easier for spirits to maneuver them because all the spirit needs to do is manipulate the wind. You can of course decorate it with statuary of your belief system and other associated tools, too, so feel free to exercise your creativity. In addition to items, it is wise to keep in mind what I said about symbols in chapter six. You may find it very useful to decorate your space with holy symbols that you work with on a regular basis so that the spirits that show up can use them to convey messages in addition to your other skills. This entire section is up to you, so feel free to explore it. You will most likely find that over time your tastes change, and when that happens, it is quite natural to redecorate as you see fit. When doing so, keep in mind what we have discussed before when it comes to what materials hold a vibration the longest. Also keep this in mind when you are setting up your chamber initially.

To a large degree, you are in control of almost everything in your dedicated spirit chamber, and it is wise to record baseline settings in your journal before doing any spirit work as a general practice. Do your best to leave no stone unturned or ignored. For example, if the thermostat is set on seventy degrees, pay attention to whether or not it fluctuates during the session. Even subtle nuances like the flickering of a candle's flame can provide great insight into the spirit and the nature of the contact. This also addresses colors, too. If you notice colors that are not normally in your room during a contact session, make a note of it. I'm sure you get the picture here, and I want to stay focused on a planned session, so I will leave the rest of this up to you.

Let's turn our attention to how the session itself actually plays out when it is occurring in your chamber. The first thing to know is that because it is your space, you are the one in the driver's seat. This can be important if you are dealing with spirits that have strong wills, and may bring up a doubt in your mind. There is no room for doubt in your spirit contact work. If you doubt, you are cracking open the door to fear, which lowers your vibration. Yes, when you are starting out, of course this is something that every medium goes through, so to doubt yourself early on is all part of the learning process. However, if you get hung up on doubt, you will not reach your full potential, so it is wise to do with it what you can. You shouldn't feel rushed to become confident, but by that same token, you should take your time and learn the right way. This is where the true value of the spirit chamber comes into play. If you practice in the same room that you use for contact, your psychic skills go into their muscle memory mode, and it helps to calm the nerves and to relax into it. When you are relaxed, you are more open and receptive to the spirits, and thus results are better than if you're tense. This is part of the muscle memory and self-hypnosis that I mentioned before. We associated our spirit chamber with safety and empowerment, and because of this, we are putting forth our best effort.

Earlier I mentioned the fly-on-the-wall metaphor, and here I would like to address it a little more in depth. When you extend your senses to contacting another being, you are allowing it to enter your mind. After all, that is the whole point of mediumship. However, you are the one that decides how much it will be in your mind. You don't have to allow complete residency, but rather you do have control over how much it comes in. The way that this occurs is that when you let it in, you establish boundaries. Yes, dealing with spirits is just like dealing with people in that if we use the same rules of conversation and etiquette with spirits that we use with each other, we can achieve a lot of success. One of the things this does is shows the spirit that you are mature enough to handle the situation, and are open enough to listen to what they have to say. Thus you allow it a certain freedom while in your physical form. Usually this freedom covers speaking through you and sharing images in your brain while you are channeling, but you may also find it wise to occasionally allow it control over parts of your body or your body overall. After you establish boundaries, you can allow your waking conscious mind to step back and let the spirit have the control you agreed on. This continues throughout the session, but there is one final point to emphasize here, and that is that ultimately, *you are the one in control*! I say this because one of the best defenses you have at your disposal if necessary is your ability to kick it out of your head if it comes down to it. Some people may think that this is not realistic because there are spirits out there "that are more powerful than we are." Really? The last time I checked, there is no part of me that is not of the gods, which means that they are not stronger than we are, but because of societal programming we are led to believe they are, but that is simply not true. Trust in your own power and trust in the training. When you do, you can easily handle the next section of this chapter.

Spontaneous Mediumship

Whereas the previous section discussed the spirit chamber, this section will discuss how to handle mediumship events if they occur when you are out and about on any given day. In a lot of ways, this is the more challenging form of mediumship because when you are confronted with a spirit outside of your spirit chamber, your comfort zone is not present, and thus it can be a challenge if you are used to your regular environment.

Earlier I mentioned that part of the continual use of your

spirit chamber is that it creates a type of muscle memory that can be very useful. However, we can't live in our spirit chamber 24 hours a day, seven days a week, can we? I'm sure you may think it would be nice to do so, but we live in a highly integrated society, so this really isn't likely. Because of this, we have to venture out from time and time, but on these ventures, the likelihood of meeting the spirits goes up in direct proportion to the amount of energy and work you've poured into your practice on a regular basis. This is important to realize because it tells us we are highly likely to encounter spirits when we are out and about. When this happens, we may get caught off guard the first few times because it's something different that we were not prepared for. I've known several people over the years that have had a hard time meeting spirits while out and about because they don't feel comfortable or confident since this isn't happening in their spirit chamber. I've even known one or two that actually go into anxiety attacks, so extreme reactions are possible. However, it doesn't have to be this way, and really that sort of reaction is mentally and energetically unhealthy. However, there is something to be said for the hesitancy that is created the first few times this is encountered. It can give an intense pause for thought, and can make us question our strength and abilities, so it is something to prepare for in advance.

Let's look at the scenario: You're on the sidewalk to the grocery store, and you suddenly get the sense that a spirit is around, and attempting to communicate with you. This can take us aback, and understandably so, especially if the spirit looks worse off or different than the ones we are used to interacting with, and this may cause us to recoil at first. When we're not in our spirit chamber, we have little to no control over the type and appearance of spirits we may encounter. This means that we can be startled the first few times it happens, and that is perfectly okay. What matters is our response to the situation, how we interact with them, and how we apply what we have learned going forward into new situations.

We may feel caught off guard because we are not in our regular environment, and we may feel off guard because our mindset is not focused on spirit contact, but regardless of how we feel, the spirit is still there in front of us, wanting to communicate. So, before we have a knee jerk reaction of fear, let's take a critical look at the situation. I'm going to break it down point by point so that this is clear, and the list can double as a brief question and answer list to be consulted later, if necessary.

Q: Why am I seeing this spirit?
A: As you have already deduced, it is because you have developed your skills to the degree that you are now a beacon for spirits in your general vicinity. As we develop psychically, we shine brighter on the other side to other spirits, and we pique the curiosity of some. However, a second reason that you are seeing it is because your gatekeeper spirit guide has allowed it through, which means that there's not much to fear from it at all. This is an important point to remember because sometimes spirits can look quite scary, especially if they are earthbound spirits that have been around for centuries or millennia.

Q: I don't have any of my normal accessories or tools with me. Can I still conduct spirit contact?
A: Yes, yes you can! All of the psychic muscle memory you've been developing is still firmly implanted in your subconscious and/or your conscious mind. Thus, the skill is still within you. What's truly missing from the equation is your comfort zone; nothing more, nothing less. You can work without comfort. This doesn't mean you have to like it though, and because of this, some mediums will still wear or keep crystals or other tools on them in a portable fashion. However, this is not necessary in any way, shape, or form, so if you want to, then go for it, but don't feel compelled to do so. Catch your breath, and proceed as if you were in your spirit chamber.

Q: Since it's not "confined" in my spirit chamber, can it hurt me, or do the odds go up for it to hurt me?
A: No, and no. Well, not directly. Yes, it could still do things like scare other people in a way that might injure you, but that's so rare, I've only heard of it happening once or twice over almost thirty years, so the likelihood of it happening to you is slim to none. You are just as much in control now as you are in your spirit chamber. This is a point I cannot emphasize enough! All

that is different is the scenery and the approach to the spirit; everything else is the same as it is in the spirit chamber. Why, you ask? Remember earlier in this book I discussed your astral temple? When you're out and about and randomly meet a spirit, your alchemical imagination takes your astral self to your astral temple, and that is the same no matter where you physically are. Your astral temple is untouchable, and because of this, it is always as strong as when you are in the spirit chamber. Your astral core is the same strength wherever you are, so it can be relied on as a sort of seat of power, which it is. When this is remembered, any misgivings or hesitations can easily fall by the wayside. Boundaries, boundaries, boundaries! Remember the law of attraction. If you are approaching this work from a space of a high vibration like love, then there is absolutely nothing to fear.

Q: This spirit doesn't look anything like ones I've encountered before. What does this mean? Should I be concerned?
A: No, not at all, even if they look very sinister and scary. Remember, a spirit can choose what it looks like, so some will choose a fierce looking appearance for various reasons. Most spirits that are earthbound humans generally do not do this though, so you don't have to really worry about that. Usually this is something that is done by a spirit that has a hidden agenda, and that is from the lower astral subplanes, so they are of a low vibration. Even then, it is wise to simply make note of its appearance, and to meditate on it later when you have the time. The only exception to this is that you may see a spirit that resembles a skeleton or a decomposing body, and this is completely natural. When it comes to appearances, there are many that you will encounter over the course of time, and their appearance is based on a few concepts. Some spirits that were human will appear to you as they prefer to be remembered, so grandmother may look like a teenager, as an example. Others have been here so long they only appear as skeletons. Some will appear as rotting corpses, and others will appear as they did at the point of death. Some will be dressed in what they were wearing at the time of their death, yet others will be dressed in clothes that they remember enjoying in life. Other spirits, particularly those that are of a more elemental nature, may

appear strange to our sight at first, but this does not mean they are bad in any way, shape, or form. We should discuss something else here at this point, and that is that the environment we find ourselves in when we have these spontaneous encounters has a tremendous impact on the type of spirits we may encounter. For example, if we are in the woods or the wilderness, we can expect more elemental type spirits, whereas if we are near a graveyard, we can expect more spirits that were once human, so we should be aware of our surroundings. As a matter of fact, it has been said many times before that the first step towards cultivating psychic development is awareness in general. When we leave our residence, we should pay attention to what is in our environment because we may find ourselves in a place where there are multiple cemeteries, which means we are more likely to encounter spirits there than in a concrete parking lot that was once a grass meadow.

The biggest challenge of spontaneous mediumship is quite honestly the first few times it occurs. After that, confidence is built, and you quickly discover you can proceed like normal. This can make for awkward situations though, especially if they show up when you least expect them. Sometimes this requires tact, as you may be attending a business meeting and one shows up to make conversation. Yes, most spirits that you will have spontaneous contact with are contacting you to pass along a message or ask for assistance of a certain kind, so it would be wise to communicate for the sake of hearing rather than communicating for the sake of being heard. In any event, they may show up almost anywhere, so it is wise to be alert but not overly obsessive, either. Sometimes discretion is the better part of valor, and to this point, keep in mind that just because a spirit is seeking contact doesn't mean you have to give it attention. There have been numerous times in my life where I deferred spirit communication because I was dealing with something on the physical world that required my immediate and thorough attention. Again, I say boundaries. No is always an acceptable answer, especially if you are dealing with things that have to do with your survival and well-being.

Once you get a handle on how to work with spirits that

appear simultaneously, you really begin to unfold because it means you can practically channel on command. This can be quite a valuable skill to develop, and I encourage everyone that is reading this to do so. However, this is not something for everyone either, so use your best discretion. I know many mediums that are quite content to channel at home, but won't do it out in public, and that is okay. Where I live now is in the middle of a triangulation of three cemeteries, so I get quite a bit of spirit traffic, both in my chamber and without, so spontaneous mediumship is something I deal with a lot, and I can tell you from experience that boundaries are really your saving grace. The second point that is your saving grace is your energetic cleansing techniques. I have found the most versatile ones are those that you memorize so that if you're out and about, you are not hindered by not having comfortable tools. Of course tools are always nice to have and use, but you can achieve success without them.

Mental discipline is the key to success here, as I'm sure you've figured out, and I re-emphasize it here because an esoteric reason for this is that you are shifting your consciousness to the mental plane, and for most spirits you encounter, this is enough of a shift to make sure you have the high ground when dealing with them. Most of the spirits you may randomly encounter are of the physical or astral planes, which means that a strong mind is enough to maintain the high ground of protection and clarity when dealing with them. Many of the human spirits you may encounter are still here because they have an emotional attachment to this world as we know it, and thus they thrive off of emotions. This is also why they generally have a message for us, or for others that they want to reach through us.

Let's play devil's advocate for a second, though, and look at very rare instances for the sake of clarification. Let's say you have a spontaneous spirit contact, and it is a nagging, stubborn spirit that won't go away. First of all, default to your energy cleansing techniques, but if you want something more, then mentally shift from the mental plane to the spiritual plane. It is at this level that it is very easy to invoke your deity for assistance if you choose. Invoking a deity into you, albeit temporarily, is always something that can be relied on to help with the situation, but this invocation should be a last resort and not a first option. If it is a first option, then you never truly develop your skills because you are constantly relying on your deity to do the work for you, so it's actually working against you. It's also mentally causing a codependent relationship with the deity as well, for the same reason. When you have the opportunity, rely on yourself first and foremost. The road to self-empowerment can be of great assistance when it comes to spirit communication, and this is especially true of spontaneous spirit contact as well. The more assured you are of your abilities, the wider the range of energetic beings you can communicate with. However, the challenge that comes with this is that you don't want to get too arrogant or cocky in your skills. We all have limits, and there are no exceptions. As has been said many times in occult circles, "hubris has been the downfall of many a good magician."

Chapter 8: Relationships

Let's turn our attention to the relationships that these spirit contact sessions can produce. I have not seen a book on this particular facet, but then again, I also haven't seen every book, so there may or may not be resources out there that address this, but if there are, they are few and far between, which is why I chose this subject for the chapter. Little to no light has been shed on this part of mediumship, save one focal point, which is ancestor worship and interaction. Several traditions out there have an emphasis on working with the ancestors in one form or another, and it may be easy to find the background information unique to your path, so feel free to do your research and to use this material to enhance it. The only particular point to remember is that they are, for the most part, working specifically with ancestors, and thus are limited to *only* ancestors. In this chapter I am going to discuss the nature of relationships with various kinds of spirits in addition to ancestors that you may encounter.

The first and most important point to note is that relationships with spirits are just like relationships with people! If you would treat the average person with respect, then treat spirits the same way. In old aeon grimoires we find this theme of "do this or God will punish you," and that is a horrific thought to ponder, is it not? That's like a toddler telling someone "Be nice to me or I'll tell my mommy!" At best it's a human throwing a temper tantrum, at worst it's emotional abuse. Are there spirits out there that would respond to such words? Of course there are, but if you go into every mediumship session with that attitude, then things will go poorly, and you may find your emotional body suffers as well, for that behavior causes a drop in vibration. If we continually threaten spirits, then we can expect lower quality and lower vibration spirits to come to our door, since we are emitting a lower vibration. It's simple karmic law of attraction. Besides, that is a very emotionally charged attitude to take with spirits, and spirits that are above the astral plane won't take well to being treated like that. An important point to keep in mind when dealing with spirits is that the higher vibration the spirit, the more finely tuned of an energy it is, and in a lot of ways, it is more fragile, meaning that it has no problem leaving if toxic behavior like that is thrown their way. Yes, there are times that form of communication can be considered, but as a general rule of thumb? No way!

If you make contact with a nature spirit, for example, then communicate with it in a manner that is appropriate to their paradigm. You wouldn't necessarily treat them the same way you would treat a spirit of the water, for example. Remember your elemental correspondences for reference points, and you should be able to navigate relationships you find yourself in. If they are humans that have now transitioned to the land of the dead, then keep that in mind, too. You wouldn't speak to the ghost of a 1950's housewife the same way you would speak to a ghost that was the CEO of a company. Common traits can still be practiced, such as respect, courtesy, etc., but to get detailed information out of them, it takes detailed questions, and these questions can only be formulated by knowing the industry they were involved in while in physical form. This is the application of the knowledge we were discussing earlier. It is not enough to increase our knowledge base; we must also put that knowledge into practice. Other than the fact it provides the spirit comfort, it also establishes a rapport of trust, and through this trust, a continual relationship is built.

That's the million dollar question though, isn't it? How do you want this relationship to go? Do you want it to be a continual relationship, or is this a one-time communication, with maybe a follow through session or two? A lot of this you will have to address off the cuff, as you may not know from spirit to spirit, but it is wise to ponder these questions now so that you don't get caught off guard. Some spirits we communicate with will only be in our lives for a very brief period of time, while others, such as our spirit guides, will be with us much longer. Leaving a spirit with a good impression of you is a wonderful thing to do, but then again there are those spirits out there that this cannot be done with, so there is that to consider. I know many people that work with the beings known as the faerie folk, and the nature of their relationships is one of an ongoing type, so those relationships are built up over years, and hence they take a lot more work than relationships with spirits that will only be around for the next few months or so.

The type of spirit in question is one of the biggest, if not the biggest, determining factor when it comes to answering these and related questions. If you are contacting a spirit that was once a human, you can relate to it in human terms, but if you are dealing with a spirit that has never been human, then it is wise to figure out just what it is, and address it accordingly. Not every spirit out there has been catalogued throughout history, so you will invariably meet spirits that you can find no reference material for, and when this occurs, contextual clues can be used to provide keen insight into their nature. For example, you may find that you meet a strange, porous, black creature when you are on a trip to an island paradise, and it leaves you stumped until you remember that the island has a dormant volcano on it! Then it becomes clear that it is related to the volcano in some way, shape, or form, either as an earth elemental, a fire elemental, or a mixture of the two, since that can happen. You can apply this same methodology to whatever environment you find yourself in, so be perceptive and inventive when trying to discern all of this. Listen to your intuition, but lead with your head.

Motives are powerful things to think about as well, both the spirit's motives and your motives. If your motives are pure and true, the type of spirit you will encounter will be much different than the kind of spirit that someone who is of dubious character will encounter. Of course the obvious rule of thumb here is to keep your motives as pure as possible to attract and interact with the best quality spirit you can, but I know some that will be reading this won't necessarily share that view, but you can still use this general rule of thumb when interacting with them. Let's look at the motives of the spirits, though. They are not always on the surface. The majority of them are, though, which is a good thing. When you encounter them, it is always wise to assess where they may be coming from, which requires the continual study of metaphysics and mediumship work. When you can easily spot spirits and can deduce what their motives are, you are in a much more empowered position to work with them. A general rule of thumb is what you may think it is: the higher vibrational the spirit, the purer their motives. Higher vibrational spirits do not care for such things as dubiousness, for they are made of finer material and have their sights set on higher values and agendas.

The good news is that if you're interacting with the spirit of someone that was once human, they are going to have human motivations, and thus they can be easier to deal with. However, if the spirits you are dealing with have never had a human life, they can be a little harder. If we know what motivates people in form in general, we can easily adapt this to the spirit world. For example, we know that most parents are protective of their children, and thus we can expect the same when it comes to interacting with people that are now in the spirit world. It gets tricky, though, when we interact with spirits that were never human because they have an almost alien consciousness, so their motives may be ones that we haven't encountered before when dealing with humans. At this point it is also wise to interject with the reminder that time doesn't exist once you drop physical form, and because of this, their understanding of time and ours are two totally different scales. For example, when they say "soon," it could mean a year from now, because that is soon to them. Hence we are reminded to be specific when we are contacting spirits, especially if time frames are being discussed. Another piece of good news is that we are generally going to be able to tell what their motives are. If you're interacting with a spirit that was once human, they generally have a message of some kind to convey as we have discussed, and we can also be fairly confident that the message is something that has to do with love, the family, or some other subject that they were passionate about. An occult axiom should be kept in mind here though, and that is that just because a being is in the spirit world doesn't necessarily mean they have all of a sudden become enlightened! This is a rule that I have yet to see an exception to, and is a powerful thought to keep in mind. This is true of all spirits, not just the ones that were human. Not having a corporeal body does not mean that they know it all. A lot of the information that they know is based on what kind of spirit they are. They have specialties, just like humans do, and because of this, they are usually good in one area and weak in another. For example, if I was interacting with the ghost of a banker, I would not necessarily discuss exercise with it, unless I knew the person had an interest in that when they were alive.

And that's the thing, isn't it? Regarding spontaneous

mediumship specifically, we generally don't know any details about the individual until after the fact, if at all, and thus we find emphasized the ideas I've been discussing: respect, curiosity, kindness. It is radically different from prepared mediumship in that when you are in your spirit chamber and are going to do spirit work, there is generally a spirit that is sought, or one that has been worked with for a long period of time. This means that there is a relationship present, and that there are correspondences that are known about to assist us in the initial contact. These correspondences and thoughts can be looked at ahead of time to prepare us for what to expect, so we have preconceived notions and thoughts, but when we are engaging in spontaneous mediumship, we do not have that set up to begin with, and because of this, we may be back on our heels initially when it comes to dealing with them. This doesn't mean a relationship can't be established, but rather we are simply caught off guard and have to adapt.

The keen mind will notice that this is just like real life, in that we're not always in complete control of those we will meet. Oftentimes we have to adapt to the situation we find ourselves in, and we have to take things on the fly, trusting our intuition. The more I study metaphysics and the deeper I make my connection with spirit, the more I come to see that it is such a strong mirror of the physical world it is uncanny. This can be very useful to know because it can help us navigate our relationships and interactions a lot better than if we thought we were doing guesswork. When we keep this basic concept in mind, we come to find that we know more about the spirit world than most people, and this can fill us with a strong sense of confidence. This confidence raises our vibration automatically, and as that occurs, it opens us to higher vibrational beings, and keeps us from lower vibrational ones.

This brings us to the concept of limits, and while so far in this book we've been talking about human limits, let's take a moment to address the limits of spirits. Yes, they have limits, even though you may meet some that say they don't. There are limits to what they can do, and there are also limits to how much they can control their vibration. This is one of the keys to testing your spirits. Spirits that tend to be on one extreme end or the other of the vibratory scale are limited to where they can go.

Very high vibrational spirits cannot go to the densest lower vibrational end of the scale, and the same is true in the opposite direction. What this means on a practical level is that as we raise our vibration, we naturally vibrate away from lower vibrational energetics. The easiest parallel to consider is this one: When we are young, we sometimes find ourselves in dangerous environments dealing with people that are not so nice, but as we grow and mature, our discernment skills improve (if we're doing things right!), and we tend to avoid those places and those people to the degree that it begins to occur naturally and subconsciously. Eventually we find that those places and people are simply fading memories, leaving us with reminders of what happens if we don't pay attention to the environments and people in our lives. This same principle is true of spirit contact, and by applying what we have learned, we can safely navigate the vibration scale. This also means that we less have to worry about certain kinds of spirits, based on where we're at on the vibratory scale. If we find we are at one particular frequency, we can deduce there are some beings that we won't encounter on average.

There are also other limits that spirits have, that Hollywood and society have embellished to the extreme that this is often embedded in our subconscious without our realization. The first limit are their powers. They do not have powers on the physical plane like superheroes, so we can be rest assured of safety from that. While they may employ powers like that on the astral plane, keep in mind that you, too, are much more powerful on the astral plane, so it becomes a moot point. When dealing with spirits and their interactions with the physical world, it is wise to keep this in mind because without realizing it, we could accidentally scare ourselves, which does no good to anyone, and works against us in the long run. I've already spoken about possession, so I won't go back to it here, but the other powers one can imagine are simply not there on the physical plane. This would violate natural law. So, what powers *do* they have on the physical plane? Quite a few, actually, and they are as subjective and varied as the stars in the sky. A general rule of thumb is that their main powers have to do with their correspondences, so if you are seeking out a particular spirit, then you know what to expect, but through deductive reasoning, you can ascertain what to expect when dealing with them. For the most part, their powers have to do with influencing others, or being opportunists for things that are already in motion. For example, some spirits can influence some peoples' minds, whereas elemental spirits can influence the element they belong to. I've had air elementals bring wind gusts out of nowhere, fire elements ignite fire, and then show up in the flames, and those are just two ideas that stand out in my mind! This is why identification is so important, and is a reiteration of why critical thinking skills are so important as well. Some spirits will tell you they can perform this, that, or the other, but it has been my experience that every time I've called their bluff, I've found them lacking.

Here's a scenario to illustrate how something plays out. Let's say you have a spontaneous channeling event that brings you into contact with a spirit that is not so nice, but your intuition tells you, you can handle it. The spirit makes the threat that it will shrink you. Of course this doesn't come to pass, but mentally and psychologically you may feel disempowered, or not quite up to snuff for a while afterwards. This would be the result of the spirit influencing your mind, but unable to do anything physically to you. To alleviate those lingering feelings, stay up on your daily upkeep and energetic cleansing techniques. This will either make the effects go away, or will at least lessen them to the degree you can ride them out. If you would have taken the spirit at face value with that empty threat, you would have reacted a lot differently, but since you knew it couldn't alter you physically, you knew you were safe on the physical plane.

This brings up a critical point about spirit contact, and that is that a vast majority of spirits use double entendres when speaking. This can be quite tedious to deal with, but I have found this to be true more often than not. A double entendre is when a word can have two very different meanings, such as in the case of the word "lead." That word has a variety of meanings, and thus to understand how it is used, we look at the context around it. The same is true when relating to the spirit world. Not only should we look at context; we should also look at the different meanings of a word or a phrase from how they may play out in life. This way, even though we may be wrong with our assessment, we are still creatively thinking, and oftentimes that is the true gem that comes from this mental exercise. Spirits are notorious through history and literature for tricking a person into something they wanted, so this alone can send shivers down our spines, but with some critical thinking instead of a knee jerk emotional reaction, we can think through our conversations with them and not be as caught off guard as we might be otherwise. If we don't know the context being used, then we should take a very careful analytical look at things to have an idea of where the spirit is coming from with it, and where the spirit wants to take it by the use of the word(s).

Oh, and by the way, that whole "selling your soul" thing? Well, um, no, for various reasons. You can't lose your soul. It's that simple. You may feel like part of it is deadened or hardened from time to time, or that it needs to get reclaimed from negativity, but you don't lose it. I guess the counterpoint to that is that if your spiritual and religious beliefs say it can be lost, then it can be, but if that is the case, then it would be wise to ask yourself why you're working with such a disempowering belief system to begin with! That is a very disempowering idea overall, and if you have this as a fear, it will negatively impact your relationship with the spirit world. The best parallel here is to think of it like this: If you were that paranoid of losing the key part of yourself in the physical world, you would never leave home and would continually walk around scared and suspicious. Yes, I know there are many, many people out there like that, but by making the choice to pick up this book and read it, you are also making the choice to better yourself overall, and to be of greater service to those that are not in a place to explore this material.

The best way I've found to interact with spirits is to think of the relationships as business transactions, with the only exception being your spirit guides, but that is a topic for another time and place. When it comes to your average run of the mill spirits, though, if you treat them professionally and maturely, you may find you have greater success than if you dip into older, more antiquated concepts. A lot of their motivations for preferring this is that they appreciate the directness. After all, as we've discussed a few times, they are contacting us to get a message across. If someone on the street in the physical world asked us for directions, they would appreciate directness, too, so why would interacting with spirits in the spirit world be any different? Getting down to business is the best way to go about things from what my experience has taught me. After all, there is no part of me that is not of the gods, and this reminds us that at our very cores, we are spirits, with the only difference being that we are encased in flesh. This also sets the stage for the time when we become spirits, as we will be treated in a like fashion from mediums we may contact, and hence it is an activation of the karmic law of attraction. If we are working in a controlled environment, this is easy to work with, because we already have an idea of what to expect from the spirit, and this includes things they may prefer. Thus we can be equipped with things they may desire ahead of time, which makes things much more expedient.

However, like physical plane relationships, there are also dangers and pitfalls to watch for when relating to spirits. The same features and concepts that apply in the physical world apply in the spirit world, so it is wise to make sure you don't become too codependent on the spirts you work with. I have seen way too many people over the years not make a move in life because they must first consult x, y, or z spirit, and while that is okay to a certain extent, it is not okay in other contexts. For example, letting your spirit pick your average run of the mill meal could be a little excessive. If it's a meal that is in exchange for services rendered, that is one thing, but if it is your average lunch while on the clock, that's another. Abusive relationships should also be avoided. These can sometimes build up so slowly they are almost insidious in nature, so they may be tricky to start off with. I once knew a woman that claimed to work with Lilith on a regular basis, and she was the member of a local goddess circle, where a group of women would get together on a regular basis and discuss and work with the feminine divine. Every year they would pick a different goddess to work with, but this woman always chose Lilith because she believed Lilith wouldn't approve. I have worked with Lilith extensively, and I can tell you from experience she is not that way. She is the vital spirit of the self-empowered and self-liberated woman. She is confident in herself and trusts herself to the degree she will go where she wants, when she wants, and will work with whom she chooses, thank you very much! True, Lilith is possessive, but it is the protective kind of possessive, and can it be jealous? Yes it can, but at the end of the day she knows where you stand, so the jealousy is passing, for the most part. There are a few lessons to take away from this story. The first one is that it probably wasn't Lilith that she was working with, but rather it was another spirit that was posing as her, which means she also didn't test her spirits, but in this case, that is neither here nor there. The second lesson to take away from this is that it is the perfect example of an addictive relationship between a physical person and a spirit. Yes, they can exist, and I have heard about so many that I feel almost compelled to write about them here.

Another type of relationship that some may encounter is that of a "spirit spouse," or some derivative term of that concept. Yes, there are people out there that marry a spirit, and while this is uncommon, it is certainly not that rare. For some people, this may be a complex idea to comprehend, so let me break it down into two basic concepts. The first concept works just like a human wedding or handfasting, in that the spirit is their spouse, and they interact with the spirit in that fashion. Usually the criteria of the agreement is stipulated ahead of time, and everything is based from a seat of love. However, another type of potentially intimate relationship with a spirit you may encounter is that of someone being pledged to a spirit, which is much different. As you can deduce from the story above, you can pledge yourself to a spirit for a particular duration. The most common duration is a year, or a year and a day, but any length of time can be used. Generally this is devotional in nature, and can produce quite a bit of personal and spiritual growth. I have done this many times throughout my magical career, and have met with positive, yet sometimes challenging, results. The best part about both of these kinds of relationships is that they are very fluid and highly subjective, so there is no right or wrong here. I simply share this information to illustrate the creativity that can be applied to your relationships with spirits. If you are seeking something intimate, then you can create it, but if you are wanting something more spiritually focused, you can create that, too! People that tell you that you can't do these things are not recognizing what you can achieve and accomplish through them, but also as mentioned above, caution and good emotional and spiritual health should be considered at all times.

Are these all of the relationships one can have with spirits? No, not at all. There are many more types of relationships one can have with the spirits they interact with, but that is all I will say on the matter because I choose to tread lightly and to do my best to avoid dogma. If you can imagine it, and the relationship is not negatively impacting your life or the life of the spirit, then by all means, feel free to explore. Oftentimes I keep things to a transaction by transaction case, but sometimes I take relationships further, just like in the physical world. If we ever doubt how to relate to a spirit, all we have to do is look at our own lives for guidance. What has worked in the past, and what hasn't? What are the majority of the relationships you have, and how do you feel about them? Are you emotionally mature in the context of the relationships? Are you being treated with respect in them? Then, if you feel a particular way about them, the spirits you will interact with will probably largely share your views on the subject, too. Not only are we now in a position to evaluate our lives for maximum growth, we are also in a position to enhance our spiritual development and the relationships we will cultivate when interacting with spirits and the spirit world.

Chapter 9: Timing

In this chapter we will discuss how to time your mediumship work, and there is a lot to be said, so let us begin. When you are first developing your psychic skills and mediumship, it is wise to pay attention to *when* you decide to work. Earlier in the book I discussed the concept of having a once a week session, if not more frequently, where you do your spirit work, and that is still true here. However, there are other factors to consider when communicating with spirits. We will look at them in depth, and I will do my best to break things down in the clearest of terms so that anyone of any educational level can understand them. I will give you a warning though, and that is that it is wise to get an astrological calendar if not a full blown ephemeris. An ephemeris is a list of placements in the zodiac for planets and other chart points that are used extensively by astrologers.

There are many facets of timing to consider, so I will break them down into three groups: 1) astrology, 2) astronomy, and 3) religious festivals. Each one can play a major role when it comes to determining when to work with spirits. Yes, especially at first, the timing of working with spirits is important to know, but as you develop, timing becomes secondary, although it truly doesn't disappear from the priorities list. It is always wise to pay attention to what is going on from a natural world perspective so that you have a better idea of what to expect regarding the results of spirit contact done under these influences.

Astrological

I know astrology can be a difficult and nebulous subject, and because of that, I write about astrology extensively in other places, and have resources available on my website for those of you that are interested. But, I can address key basic concepts here as points to pay attention to when you are deciding when to make spirit contact. The first, and most basic, are the cycles of the moon. The moon has been a source of mystery and mystique for thousands of years. Its effects on the tides and on the physical world in general are well documented and readily available to those that seek them. When it comes to the Moon, there are several points to be aware of before you decide to work with it. The magnetism of the Moon affects collections of water. The human body is composed of 75 percent water, and thus it is easy to deduce that the pull of the Moon can affect us physically. This has been corroborated by many different scientific experiments of the recent past. Crime goes up around the time of the full moon, as do trips to the emergency room and trips to the veterinarian. Psychic skills are also enhanced at this time, as there is the natural current in the air to tap into.

The cycles of the moon are easiest understood in this fashion: New Moon-1st Quarter-Full Moon-Last Quarter, then back to New Moon. So you can break this cycle down to 2 two-week cycles: when the moon is moving from new to full, and when the moon is moving from full to new. When the moon is moving from new to full, it is called the waxing moon, which also means a building of energy. Then the moon is moving from full to new; it is called the waning moon, and means a reduction of available energy.

During the waxing moon, there is more energy available to tap into, and thus certain traits may be noticed. These include such things as more aggression, perhaps sleeplessness, frenetic energy, and all things related to these adjectives. Thus, this is a good time to begin things. For example, you could begin a new workout routine. Or, perhaps, a new meditation or eating routine. Whatever the case may be, this is the time to work with the extra energy in the air. Of course, by default, the waning moon is when there is a decrease of energy in the air, and because of this, it is an excellent time for banishings, cleansings, and endings.

Every two and a half days there is also a period that occurs from the last time the moon makes a strong aspect in one sign to the first strong aspect of the next sign. This period is known as the void-of-course moon, and is often misunderstood, but can also be very potent if you choose to work with it. During these void-of-course times, there is no direct influence from the moon on us, so there is a certain energetic freedom that occurs. However, sometimes things can go haywire unexpectedly, and thus sometimes things have to be redone.

Let us move on to the next astrological point to note, which is what is called a "planetary ingress." This is far easier to explain and understand than the lunar cycles though, so we will be brief. This term references when a planet changes from one sign to another. The reason this is important is because traits and correspondences that have to do with that planet and sign combination can manifest in very different ways than you may expect. Sometimes there are challenges that come up with them. Other times manifestations happen in a much distorted fashion. The only fine point to note is that there isn't really a predetermined length of time over which this occurs, because how long this takes is based on the planet. The general rule of thumb is that the closer the planet is to the Sun, the faster the ingress period. For example, when Mercury enters into a new sign, it takes approximately a day, whereas when Saturn changes signs, it takes weeks! The lesson to take away from this is to periodically check for these occurrences because they can greatly affect your spirit contact in a number of ways.

Another astrological point to consider is when a planet moves from direct to retrograde, via a stationary period. Okay, so that sounds complicated, doesn't it? Let's start with the baseline that all planets are moving direct by default, because they are! They're moving direct in their orbits around the Sun. However, all planets travel at different rates of speed and have different orbits, so from time to time, these periods come up. First, let's understand what retrograde motion is. Retrograde motion is best understood with the following analogy, because most of us have experienced this, usually unknowingly. Have you ever passed a car on the interstate, and as you looked in your mirror or over your shoulder, you've noticed that the vehicle you passed seemed to shrink and look like it's going backwards? If you have, then you've experienced retrograde motion. Succinctly, it is when a planet seems to be going backwards and shrinking from our vantage point here on earth. Of course it is not going backwards, nor is it shrinking, but rather it is an optical illusion.

A planet doesn't just "go" retrograde, though. First it goes through a period known as "stationary." The duration of a stationary period is based on the rate of speed of the planet as outlined above, so sometimes a planet will be stationary for a few hours, whereas for other planets, they may be stationary for days. The same general rule of thumb applies here, too, so keep the fluidity of the duration in mind. One of the biggest ways this will manifest in your mediumship work is that the stationing period and the correspondences of your spirits will most likely be impacted. For example, when Saturn is stationing to go retrograde, you may find the general tone of conversations with your spirits to be more somber, serious, and mature.

Because of this different energetic, the body's influence manifests differently than on a day to day level. Planets retrograde in the sky can have an impact on mediumship work. They may produce different results and different types of spirit interactions, so it is wise to pay attention. One final thought to stress is that retrograde points are NOT negative! They are simply different styles of manifestation than direct points. Also of note is that the two luminaries, the sun and the moon, are NEVER retrograde. For example, if the moon could go retrograde, we would see its dark side! The sun and the moon represent our inherent internal masculine and feminine natures, and thus they are us at our core. They represent who we are when everything else is stripped away.

One final astrological point that I will mention here is that astrological aspects can play a major role in your spirit work. However, let's put that on the back burner for now. After all, aspects are a more advanced astrological concept at this point, and you can work around them for the moment. Yes, you can work around them later, too, but we'll cross that bridge when we get to it.

Astronomical

This is sort of a catchall category, really, and for astronomical purists, this will probably get under your skin, because I'm not going to simply address astronomy. Rather I will include other geo-astronomical phenomena because all of this should be taken into account when you are doing mediumship work.

Let's start with sunspots. Sunspots are increased activity from solar flares on the surface of the Sun. They erupt in varying strength and on a particular cycle, which is approximately eleven years. This cycle has been shown to affect the stock market, among other things, so its influence on us has been well documented, and thus I won't go into it here. I simply mention it now because sometimes sunspots can add a little spark of energy to your mediumship work. If you have a particularly intense period of mediumship, you may want to check to see if it is a period of increased solar flare activity.

Now we turn our attention to the thickness of the veil from a wheel of the year perspective. Before we discuss the veil, though, let us define the wheel of the year. In Neopaganism, the wheel of the year is the term given to the cycles of the earth, and in essence, breaks the year down into eight sections. Why eight, you ask? Four of the break points are astrological in nature. They are the two equinoxes, which are the two times of the year that the Sun crosses the equator, which are known as the times of great balancing, and one occurs in March on Spring Equinox, while the other occurs in September, at the Autumn Equinox. From a practical perspective, this is also when we have season changes, but that would require more space to discuss than I am prepared to give it here. Suffice to say, this is a time when things are brought into balance, and the way this impacts mediumship work is that oftentimes activity is increased around these points. As you can see, the two points are offset from each other by six months. These are also the beginnings of two seasons: Spring and Autumn. The next two major points are the solstices. These occur twice a year, when the Sun reaches either its strongest height in the sky, or its weakest, lowest point in the sky. When it is at its height, we have the beginning of Summer, and when it is at its lowest, we have the beginning of Winter. Solstices are opposite of each other on the two hemispheres of the planet though, so it is wise to keep this in mind if you are in contact with a spirit that is from a particular culture that is located in a different hemisphere of the planet. By the way, in this case I'm talking about the northern hemisphere and the southern hemisphere of the planet, not the eastern and the western. The same rule of thumb applies here that applies to equinoxes, in that you may find these periods greatly impact your mediumship work. The way all four of these points impact your mediumship work is that they oftentimes bring the qualities of the elements to the surface in your work, and thus you should be mindful of this when you work with the finer planes.

The other four points of the wheel of the year are located in the direct middle of those four solar ingress periods, so those are the true heights and potencies of the particular season they are located in. Every sign in astrology is thirty degrees, and these four chart points occur in the direct middle at fifteen degrees, but in the middle sign of the segment of three that constitute a season. As a general rule of thumb, this is important to realize because increased spirit activity and heightened mediumship may also be experienced as well. There are many good books on the wheel of the year, so I won't go deeper into it here, other than to say when you're evaluating the results of your spirit work, or if you experience something out of the ordinary, it would be wise to see if any of these eight occurrences are happening. While I just showed this eight spoked wheel is logically created, it has ties to many different traditions and belief systems, most of them Western European and Middle Eastern in creation, and this is the perfect segue into the final section of this chapter: the religious aspect of mediumship timing. Before we jump into that though, let's finish this section by discussing the veil between the worlds.

The concept of a veil between the worlds can be found in many different cultures across the globe, and thus, while subjective to a large extent, there are some pearls of wisdom to discover. Briefly, the concept is that there is a veil between the worlds, which is why our senses are largely limited to the physical world. The model I want to address here is largely Western European-centric, but it plays a major role in the western world. It is based on the premise that there are certain times of the year that the veil is thinner than others. The traditional concept we will generally encounter tells us that there are two points of the year that the veil is the thinnest: around Samhain, and around Walpurgisnacht. These two ancient festivals come to us from western European traditions, and are directly located opposite from each other on the wheel of the year. Samhain occurs in early November, and Walpurgisnacht occurs in early May. Traditionally, Samhain is a time to honor the ancestors and to celebrate the new energetic year as it pertained to that belief system. Walpurgisnacht is known as the night of the witches, and is the night before the ancient festival of Beltane, which celebrates life, fertility, planting seeds, and all things associated with new beginnings. To tie this in astrologically, Walpurgisnacht occurs at fifteen degrees Taurus, and Samhain occurs at fifteen degrees Scorpio. Because of this, the dates change almost every year, but these are important times to take note of because when they are present, it tells us we may have an easier time contacting spirits. Of course other cultures speak of different times of the thinness of the veil, so it is wise to do your research with your belief system to see how they handle it, but if necessary, feel free to adapt these concepts as mentioned here to your own path.

Religious

This is listed last because, in my opinion, it is the least impacting of the three criteria we're discussing here. The reason for this is because we're talking about something here that is not a natural phenomenon; rather it is created by humanity for religious reasons. However, there has been so much energy poured into these festivals over time that they have their own energetic current that can be tapped into, and when this occurs, it means you are in a perfect position to work with spirits that are part of your religious belief system.

One of the best ways I've found to work with this is to work with a particular deity on their festival day. However, another technique that is good to use is to contact your religious ancestors during this time as well. For example, on a festival day sacred to the Egyptian goddess Hathor, you may find it easier to call on her and work with her, but you may also find it easy to tap into the divine feminine, since she is one of the oldest goddesses on the planet. Another possibility is that you may find it especially easy to tap into ancient Egyptian religious ancestors you may claim as well. Oftentimes, ancestors are split into different categories, and don't necessarily have to do with flesh and blood ancestors, but rather the ancestors that came before you that work with and are part of this system.

Because of the amount of energy people through time have poured into these festivals and feast days, you may find a lot of success at your fingertips. However, something else to take note of is that you may get contacted by spirits of those particular religions during this time in a way that is stronger than at other times of the year. I have heard many cases over the years where someone was contacted by spirits from a belief system that wasn't theirs, and this usually happened when it was a religious festival that was sacred to the spirit. Although uncommon, it is something to keep in mind because it tells us that the spirits will use these windows of opportunity to make contact with a medium, and oftentimes this results in the education of a medium about a new belief system they hadn't given much thought to before. This doesn't mean the medium should automatically jump into that new belief system, but rather the medium should at least get educated about that belief system so that they can help that particular spirit out to a greater extent. This also crosses over into increasing the knowledge base of the medium, which was discussed in depth earlier in this book.

An extension of this concept is also subjective in nature, and that is that it makes the medium ask themselves what days are sacred to them. This is worth noting because it tells us that each and every one of us creates our own spiritual and religious holy days, and the more we adhere to their observance, the more we create energy ourselves for our own use. In other words, the more we work with our own festival days, the more we put energy into these patterns, and the greater the potential that is present for spirit contact. There are certain days of the year that I hold sacred, and the more I honor them and work with them, the more they bring me in terms of spirit contact. However, I'm the only one working with them to this point, so they produce limited energy, and that is quite all right, because it works for me. You can adopt the same model and concept to your own life. The main point to remember is that the only way energy gets poured into these days is through the discipline of honoring them year after year. Thus there is also a note that comes with this, and that is that in the beginning, you may not find a lot of strong results, but as time goes on, you may find results are more dynamic.

Of course all of this information implies that there is a religion you work with on a regular basis. If you don't have one, that's fine, but it would be wise to be a little more thorough when it comes to spirit contact in order to compensate. Instead of simply taking verbatim the spirit and the contact that comes with it you may find yourself paying attention to the calendar a little bit more, and studying different religions a little more in depth so that when spontaneous spirit contact occurs, you have an idea of why it is occurring. Let's look at a generic example. Let's say that someone is not Christian or part of the Abrahamic belief systems at all, but they get a visit from a spirit they don't know. They then check the calendar and see it is a festival day of one of those faiths. That would tell them then, that the spirit is associated with that faith, or at least finds comfort or strength in that faith, and thus it would be wise to get educated on those faiths, specifically the festival day that is occurring at this time in order to facilitate better contact with the spirit in general. This kind of thinking is valuable when it comes to analyzing what spirits share with us.

A detailed point to remember is that sometimes spirits will come from religions that have gone extinct, so you may not find religious correspondences. This doesn't mean the spirit doesn't have any validity, but rather if they pass the tests, they are beings you can learn from. This can really take you out of your comfort zone though, as it takes confidence to address something that is unknown to the history books. While this may make for quite the adventure, you may find it wise to be careful who you share that information with because some people will think you are not right in the head, or something related to that. There have been a few times in my life when I have come across a spirit that either had beliefs that I couldn't find references to, or they were deities that time forgot, so I can speak from experience that this can be frustrating, but the tradeoff is that you are getting insight into something that 99 percent of the planet forgot. Contextual clues and communication can reveal quite a bit, and this is worth paying attention to because something of the belief system they were a part of was absorbed into later belief systems, so you can gain a deeper understanding of how particular religions were created. This is a mental exercise in connecting the dots, and can be quite rewarding and beneficial.

A topic I don't give a title to, though, is worth a mention here, and I'm putting it under the heading of religious because there are people out there that have emotions bordering on religious for it, and this topic is nationalism. Sometimes, spirits will come to you on days that correspond to particular nations, so it is wise to watch the calendar and pay attention to those dates, too. For example, here in America in the middle of the 19th century we had a civil war. I have met a few spirits that died in that war but have not moved on yet. If I didn't know my history, I would not have been able to place them. The way they appeared to me was wearing their military outfits, so I had to be able to place the outfits, but also to know history enough to know the time era as well as which side they were serving at the time of their death. What makes this idea sometimes hard to work with is the fact that you may achieve contact with a spirit from another country, and if you don't know about that country, it may be a challenge to even get pointed in the right direction, let alone to know the details of the spirit. A thin line you may find yourself walking is the line between doing your research, and obsessing until you find the information you're looking for, so please use your best judgment. The rule of thumb I like to use is context, so for example, if it's a spirit from another nation that contacts me, but I'm in that nation temporarily, then I wouldn't do much research, but if it's a deity or some other type of entity, I may explore it a little more in depth. Perspective can also be of great help here.

Are there other worthwhile days to consider with spirit contact? Emphatically, yes, and the ideas in this chapter are simply broad ideas to keep in mind when in contact with spirits. It would be impossible to list *all* the possible reasons for a particular date, but by keeping in mind what is mentioned here, you can fine tune your analysis of spirit contact so that you can move ahead with more confidence and clarity.

Chapter **10**: Upkeep

We've now come to the end of this tome on spirit contact, and there are very few stones left unturned. However, as much as this is the conclusion of the book, it is only the beginning of the next leg of your journey. Now that you've seen things laid out carefully, you can begin to tailor make your practices to your own preferences, and when you do this, you really step into more of your personal power than if you were developing on an island by yourself. It is also wise to keep in mind that there is no one absolute book that is an authority on spirit contact, which is why I chose to focus on techniques, templates, and the like, so that as you read and develop more, you still have a working framework to use and expand on.

But really, where do you go from here? What does all of this mean in a living context? As I'm sure you've figured out, now that you have a grasp on what it means to be a medium, you are now in a position of greater power, which means that there are greater responsibilities that are attached. As has been said many times over the years, you can't walk away from this. While that may sound foreboding, it is quite honestly true. Even if you finish reading this book, work with it for a few months, and then decide to walk away from the protocols that are included, you have still worked with the material enough to change your approach to interacting with spirits, and thus your vibration will be different to reflect that.

What this means is that once you've begun this path, it is one to keep up on and to diligently work at, developing your own style as you go. You may find different techniques down the road to achieve the same results from using the ones in here, and that is okay. Adaptation is the key to evolution after all, and the more you adapt, and the more you cause your system to adapt, the more you express your individuality and personal strength. Discipline becomes key, as does humility and understanding. Something that is not mentioned enough is the benefit of using compassion when addressing spirits. Another point to be aware of is that of respect. I am the first to say that respect is earned and never given freely, but by that same token, the spirits you are interacting with are autonomous individual beings, which means that they should be thought of as such, and treated as such. They have just as much right to exist as you do, and when we are conscious of this, we can achieve a higher vibration of success. I'll also be the first to admit that it is always better to work with higher vibrational beings than not, and the best way to experience this is to continually raise your vibration in all that you do. By taking control of toxic relationships in your life, and bringing your life in line with your Will, you raise your vibration on a day to day basis, and in ways that are common to many people across the planet. While mediumship can be used to contact beings of many different vibrations, the ones that are higher are ones that are more likely to share feelings of compassion, joy, and love, whereas lower vibration beings are those that may, on average, display an entirely different set of characteristics based on where they're at on the vibration scale.

Being a medium is not a fad or a passing phase that one goes through; rather it is a way of life. I have met many people in my life that have been medicated out of being in contact with the spirit world, and in some cases this was for the best, and in others it weakened their personal power, but the one common trait among all of them is that they were not raised or educated in an environment where spirit contact and interaction were taught or developed. Let's extrapolate this for a moment. Most people that are reading this didn't come from a background where spirits and spirit contact were discussed, let alone taught, which means that the majority of people that you will meet are approaching this from that perspective. In other words, we're all in this together. In recent years there has been an increase of people that were raised with these concepts, but by and large, in older generations, the education and training simply wasn't there. I share these points of perspective because they paint the picture that you can almost never stop learning new and better techniques from those with whom you come into contact. As has been said many times, everyone we meet is our student and our teacher. Keeping an open mind when communicating with other mediums is something that can serve us well, but so can critical thinking skills. I've learned a lot about mediumship by simply mentally picking apart the mediumship of others that I have been exposed to. I haven't judged them per se, but the effect it had on me was to keep me mentally sharp. Some people don't like this approach because it means we're always "on," and that is an approach I have seen successful, too, so it is an option. Mediumship is a way of life, and because of this, we are always "on." This doesn't mean that our mediumship skills are always open to spirit contact, but rather it is wise to never let your guard down. We are always "on" stage. For example, I have heard many times from people that they are not "working with magic" at whatever moment I speak to them, but that is simply not true, magically or when it comes to spirit contact. If we're living it and doing it, then we ARE it. I just simply prefer to keep my skills almost always mentally sharp, or at least as sharp as possible. Some of this chapter will be a recap of earlier chapters, and that is my intent because I want all of this in one place so that you can use this as a reference point if you choose. In this chapter I am going to lay out the physical, emotional, mental, and spiritual plane upkeep points to be aware of going forward to bring you further success in your channeling.

Physical Plane Upkeep

This is the easiest plane to keep up on, and yet for a lot of people this is also one of the hardest because we are limited to twenty four hours a day, and we have a responsibility to our body, if nothing else, so a lot of our time is already claimed. We can work out a healthy balance though, and when you have achieved this, it can be maintained with relative ease. This doesn't mean it's easy to achieve though, and much like spending time at the gym, the hardest part of the process is getting started.

Let's begin with the diet. As I'm sure you've guessed, I'm no diet expert, so please, please, please, double check things if your intuition says I might be wrong, or that you may be the exception to the rule to what I'm writing. There are many more qualified people out there to help you with this, and the most important point is simply to make sure it gets done at all. From this point forward, your diet plays a bigger role in your life for the reasons mentioned above, so it is wise to treat it more respectfully than you were previously. Drinking plenty of water, eating fresh foods, and making sure that you have a balanced diet are all very good practices to put into place. There is something I will touch on here for a moment that I have seen discussed before, and that is the topic of vegetarianism, and how it relates to your path. There has been a lot of information that has come to light over the last few decades regarding this subject, but unfortunately that has come with a lot of dogma, too. There are pros and cons to being vegetarian, especially when it comes to relating to energy work and mediumship, and here again I say to use your best judgment. Before Eastern teachings were brought into the Western world via Theosophy, there really wasn't a lot of emphasis placed on vegetarianism, but since that time, circa late 19th century, a profound interest has been taken in becoming vegetarian. You will read in some places that it is more conducive to mediumship than being a meat eater, and quite frankly, that is not true. I have known exceptional mediums that are both vegetarian and not, and have seen no proof that one is better than the other. If being vegetarian makes you a better medium, then so be it, but if it doesn't, then so be that, too. However you decide to approach this, do your research and make the healthy choice. Your health is much more important than your mediumship work, or the propaganda that you may read in dubious sources.

Following the diet, let's address exercise, since I discussed liquids in a previous chapter. From what I've experienced, exercise is not emphasized enough when it comes to occultism and mediumship, yet it is a very integral part of the process. By taking care of your body, you are keeping your channel operating at peak performance. This doesn't necessarily mean that you have to join a fitness club to be healthy, but it does mean that activities like stretching, push-ups, sit-ups, and related activities, should be engaged in to produce the maximum results of your work. Part of exercise also means listening to your body; not just because it is your subconscious mind like was discussed before, but also because it is a more proactive way to head off health challenges before they become major situations. There are many books and resources out there that can assist you with this, so I won't spend a lot of time on it, but rather I simply want to draw your attention to it so it doesn't get neglected. As we discussed before, it is too easy to lose sight of the physical plane in pursuit of the spiritual plane, and the best way to avoid spiritual fantasy is to be engaged in the physical world in a healthy way. Getting regular doctor visits and checkups helps ensure that you're on the right track to optimal health.

Another part of the physical plane to keep in mind is the environment you inhabit. Quite frankly, we're all doing the best we can with our individual living situations, but there are a few things I would like to point out and reiterate for the sake of clarity. Some people say that living in an urban area is more conducive to spirit contact because you can devote more of your time to honing your skills, but others say it is better to live in a rural setting because you don't have to worry about all of the headaches that go along with an urban setting. I have found that one is not better than the other, and hence it is your free choice. However, there are a few points to consider. The first one is context. If you live in an urban center, then the likelihood of dealing with more rural topics (stepping in pig doo-doo when leaving your house) declines, while if you live in a rural setting, the likelihood of having a convenience store on every corner declines. One of the big reasons this is important is because the more we keep this in mind, the sharper our senses become to messages we receive. For example, if we live in a rural area but have a vivid dream of something that is usually found exclusively in a city, it is wise to interpret it differently than we normally would. The converse is also true. If we live in an urban area but have vivid dreams of rural themes, these are worth paying special attention to for various reasons as well. While I am using dreams as an example here, this kind of thinking can also apply to what we experience. For example, if you live in an urban area but see a deer when you step outside of your door, that's something extra special to pay attention to, whereas if you live in a rural setting, it's not as striking. I have known plenty of people over the years that live in an urban setting and think that every time they see a pigeon, it is an arcane message, but we know that it's not, because pigeons are urban dwelling creatures for the most part. I'm sure you see where I'm going with this. Context is created, and thus we have a clearer lens of interpretation to process through as we live life. The main thing to keep in mind for spirit contact, and really for general well-being, is to find an environment that is not toxic, where we can find peace, safety, and rest.

Emotional Plane Upkeep

The upkeep of this plane can be quite the challenge. As I'm sure many of you know, working with emotions and emotional health are two things that can take quite a lot of work and emotional pain, so this is a plane to handle with care. After you've traveled down the spirit contact road to the point that you know it is a lifestyle rather than a hobby, it is time to engage in self-love, and to handle situations that have to do with your emotions when they come up, rather than turning a blind eye to them. Yes, I'm talking about emotional health in general, but first and foremost is your personal emotional health. If you are not emotionally healthy and/or satisfied to the best of your abilities, then it is time to make some changes for the better. It is very hard to contact higher vibrational beings if your emotions are in a perpetual state of turmoil. Likewise, if you are completely detached and out of touch with your emotions, you may find it just as hard to contact higher vibrational beings. While we will look at some instances for clarification and illustration, there is much more than I could possibly address here, but the good news is that there are a lot of resources available to you to help you with whatever situation you find yourself in.

One of the reasons we come into physical form is to be engaged in life in all of its pursuits and pleasures. Yes, earlier I said that detachment is key, but this should be tempered with the point that if you're always detached, you're never really enjoying life, and existence is pure joy, so there is a lot that is missed out on. Being engaged in life as an active participant cannot be stressed strongly enough. We are here to enjoy the fruits of this world, and what this does for us, other than enriching our lives, is put us in touch with the physical world we inhabit, which means that our palette is increased for spirit contact. The more we experience, the more we can relate to the experiences of spirits. Having said that though, as the great poet William Blake said, "The road of excess leads to the palace of wisdom," and hence there is something to be said for knowing your limits. Our experiences are what make us human, and through this we come into closer contact with spirits and the spirit world because they have had many experiences too, and thus we can relate to them in a better fashion than if we stay secluded and choose not to engage in the world around us.

However, we should temper this idea with intelligence, wisdom, and practicality. Being a thrill-seeker and adrenaline junkie may be fun, but it is like being an addict to a destructive substance as well, so it is wise to know when to say stop, or no. What does this have to do with emotional health and upkeep, you may be thinking? If we're constantly pushing ourselves, we never stop and smell the roses, and this works against us because we never take time to appreciate what we have. Appreciation and gratitude are two of the best traits to cultivate as we personally develop, and while on the surface this may seem like I'm talking about very advanced topics, the fact of the matter is that if we don't engage in appreciation and gratitude, and we don't stop periodically, we are not really addressing our emotional state in a positive way, but rather we are constantly psychologically and emotionally on the run, so in some cases we are running from facing the reality around us. That is just about as unhealthy as it comes. Denial, and running away from problems, are two of the worst courses of action we can take, and the emotional body is the one that receives the damage the worst. Of course a lot of times our emotions are the cause of this running, which brings us to the next point.

If you want to work with the spirit world in its full spectrum, it is wise to be as emotionally healthy as you can be. If you suffer from codependency, or other maladies of emotions, then higher vibrational entities may be hard to contact. Quite frankly, it's the idea that if you as a medium don't have it together emotionally, then how can they expect you to have it together when you attempt to converse with them? Yes, they are there for our contact in times of duress and stress, but if that is the only time you call on them, then there's a problem. Codependency, abuse, addictions, abusive addictive relationships, and all matters of emotional unhealth are to be addressed to the best of your abilities before attempting to contact spirits on a regular basis. This also crosses intro controversial territory because it addresses situations like grief, sorrow, and healing, and there are some out there that say something to the effect of "who are you to say when someone should be healed from grief?" The good news is that I'm not making that claim at all. We all heal and address our emotional situations in line with our individual paths, so for another to judge that is wrong. However, there are some basic concepts to note to help create a baseline. The first is that if your emotions and emotional situations are inhibiting your life in an unhealthy and dangerous way, then it's time for a change for the better. Oftentimes, people identify with their unhealthy emotions because it's more comfortable than addressing them, and thus they take the easy way out. I get that, I really do. After all, as we discussed earlier, the energy flow through the multiverse follows the path of least resistance, so to take the lazy and comfortable way out only makes sense from an energetic perspective. However, as Dr. Jung observed, "There's no coming to consciousness without pain," so if we want to advance and grow, then it is wise to take the more challenging road from time to time. This is an endeavor that is not ignored by beings on the higher planes, by the way, because they see the effort, and if you call on them during those times, many of them are more than willing to help. As far as the healing process of grief goes, I'm going to speak very little about it because I have been surrounded by death since I was very young, so my views are quite different than the rest of society in general, and there are situations that I also simply can't relate to because I haven't experienced them. For example, as of the time of this writing I have not had any children, so to me there's no way I could truly address the grief of a parent that lost a young child. However, there is a model that I came across that I have found to be a useful, albeit rough, guideline to follow and adapt. Dr. Elisabeth Kübler-Ross wrote a famous book on death and the grieving process[5], and as I've gotten older, I've learned to appreciate it more and on deeper levels. For those of you that may have grief to deal with, I encourage you to check it out because it has been of use to me. In short, there are stages and timelines that go with the grieving process, and it is wise to understand them. While the book breaks them down into numbers and stages, I have also found that these are general rules of thumb rather than absolutes, so if your experiences are slightly different from a chronological order, then so be it. Grieving, and healing, are

---

[5] Death, the Final State of Growth, by Elisabeth Kübler-Ross

gradual processes that we go through; they are not absolutes, and all of this is relevant here because while the book is focused on death, I have found it almost as useful when it comes to other emotional wounds we may suffer, so it is quite versatile. Beyond death and grieving though, there are plenty of resources out there that can help you with whatever emotional situation(s) you may be dealing with. For now, simply know that if they are not dealt with, your ability to communicate with spirits and the spirit world will be greatly limited, and may even result in emotional, psychological, and spiritual sickness.

Mental Plane Upkeep

In some ways, this is the hardest plane to work with on a continual basis, and in others it is the easiest. On one hand, staying up on the mental plane is something that can be done by increasing our knowledge and wisdom on various subjects. This is an easy way to stay engaged on your mental plane upkeep. However, a more challenging part of it has to do with staying in control and in touch with your emotions. Another part of this has to do with boundaries, logic, reason, and rationale. I read a lot of material on how to handle emotions and emotional situations, but there is far less written out there to address mental plane issues and subjects - at least not on the surface. I have yet to find a book or resource that addresses mental abuse under one cover in a format that matches addressing emotional abuse in one cover, as an example. But, bingo, that's it. You see, when you're looking for mental plane upkeep tools, it's actually easier to find what you're looking for than it is to address emotional situations. The trick lies in being specific with what you want to learn. For example, when you're looking at keeping up with your mind and mental plane, you can focus in on one particular subject or area, only to discover that whatever subject you want to know more about is already written about extensively. For example, let's say you want to learn robotics so that you can make contact with scientists now in spirit. All you have to do is research robotics in depth. I point this out because there are very few books out there, if any, that are called "The Mental Plane 101," so at first it may seem frustrating, but when you keep this simple observation in mind, you will have access to a lot more than you may have thought in the beginning, and even arguably more than if you were researching emotional plane situations, since the study of them is fairly new to our species in modern history.

Boundaries and other related mental health concepts do require a little more attention, though, because it's not like you can find a "Boundaries for Beginners" book, either. A lot of times these subjects are found when you are researching emotional health subjects, but this can still seem a bit of a challenge. The basic rule of thumb for boundaries is simple: "No means no." That's it at its essence, but of course there is a lot more to it than that. These are spirit *beings* that you are interacting with, after all, which should not be forgotten. Psychology can be of great assistance with what we're discussing here, and anything having to do with mental health. The more you maintain a healthy lifestyle with regards to your mind, the better off you'll be when it comes to interacting with spirits and the spirit world. It is wise to make sure you don't have any of a number of mental conditions, such as varying psychoses and "-enias," and this goes above and beyond self-diagnosing. There is a time and a place for that, but before beginning and continuing your mediumship development, you may want to go a little deeper than self-diagnosis. However, as always, use your best judgment when determining your course of action.

Let's use a hypothetical situation to illustrate a point rooted in the physical world, and let's say that you do have a psychological condition, but you have chosen not to address it in a healthy and proper fashion. I know it happens, especially in this culture of hyper focus and constant on the go motion, so let's look at how to really handle it. The first step to take is to put your mediumship work on the back burner until the situation is handled. Failure to do so puts you and your loved ones as risk, quite literally. The other danger that is tied to this is personal mental and spiritual trauma that can be produced from this lack of control. If you have a mental condition as illustrated above, it is far easier to fall into the realm of spiritual fantasy without realizing it, and while this is good in small doses (welcome to the land of the muse for the creative types reading this), it can also be easy to get lost in it as well, much to your detriment. In brief (yes, I realize this is an extreme illustration), this can open the door to the road of madness, and sometimes you cannot come back from that.

This is the reason mental upkeep is almost imperative. The more your practice is rooted in practicality and health, the better off you are. The more you stay grounded while communicating with spirits, the better off you are in the long run because your mediumship should be an enhancement to your life, not a way to escape from it. Oftentimes we can be quite emotionally and spiritually fulfilled by doing this work in the name of service to humanity, but this is something that can take a while to cultivate. I have helped more than one earthbound spirit cross over to where they needed to go in my life, and I know some mediums out there that specialize in this very subject, so the potential to make a difference in the existence of a spirit for the better is there, and can help both you and the spirit personally develop.

Spiritual Upkeep

This is another topic that has been written extensively about, so I won't go over the same material again, but this is where the color really gets added to things. A large part of this has to do with your daily spiritual discipline. By integrating your spiritual and religious beliefs into your day to day life, you bring yourself in tune to the living energies around you. However, you also cultivate a deeper level of connection and personal power as well.

Your spiritual upkeep when it comes to mediumship work is how you handle your faith on a day to day basis. Rituals like sun salutations, daily energy cleansings, and meditations, are all points to consider, but if you've walked a spiritual and religious path for a while, you already have access to a lot of this. How you create your daily practice, and what all is in it, is up to you. The main point to consider here is that of discipline, so when putting a daily practice together, remember to put it into context of your day to day life so you don't accidentally overwhelm or burn yourself out. I have seen many people over the years deplete their energy in this way, so I know it can happen, and I also know it can happen accidentally, when your attention may be on acquiring more and more and more. Sometimes daily spirit contact and mediumship work is chosen, but other times once a week spirit contact is chosen, and both are equally valid. When I was being taught, I was taught to cultivate a once a week spirit night where you train your guides and teachers, and in this case other spirits, to speak with you then, so you can think of it as medium office hours, in a way. However, I also moved past this to a daily practice, but I know that is not the case or preference for a lot of people, so do what thou wilt shall be the whole of the law. Both ideas are valid, and as you can see, both are subject to change when life demands it.

In modern times, a lot of discussion is occurring on the idea of exclusivity versus eclecticism, and I will touch on that debate here, but will also ignore it for the most part. There are pros and cons to both, and it is wise to use your best judgment, rather than to blindly follow what someone else says. There is much value in finding a system and adhering to a system, but there is much value in taking the best from multiple systems and making them all your own. Use what works for you, but there are a few critical thinking points to note.

The first point is that the more eclectic you become, the more your energy is scattered across different belief systems and paradigms, so you want to make sure to not spread yourself too thin. The second point to note is that the wisdom of the movie *Ghostbusters* can come into play as well, and that is "Don't cross the streams." Some pantheons and paradigms can be used to great positive effect, but there are also some that you don't want to cross, either. The easiest way to avoid crossing streams that conflict is to do your research and to use your best judgment. Have you noticed how this is a reoccurring theme? This is because a large part of your best judgment is how in touch you are with your subconscious and intuition, and those two ideas are subjective to you.

Initiations and aligning yourself with particular entities and energies of a given pantheon (or a few) is something to also be mindful of. When you initiate into a spiritual and religious tradition, you bring yourself in alignment with that belief system and culture. That means that you take on the karma of it as well, and since an initiation is to begin your devotion and practice associated with that belief system, it is wise to know what you're getting yourself into early on so that you don't accidentally take on too much karma of an unintended nature. Every belief system out there has its karmic baggage, much like people, and thus when we prepare to initiate into something, we should be mindful of the spiritual and energetic backlash that may come with it.

Like I said at the beginning of this section, this is a little briefer than the other planes because a lot is available to you, and really this is a personal decision and journey to be made. Like the rest of this book, I simply offer up these points for consideration. As you move forward with your relationship with spirits and the spirit world, you will find that as you grow and change, so too do your religious and spirit contact practices, and that is quite all right. After all, stagnation equals death, which I'm sure you will notice with the type of spirits that you interact with. Resting on the laurels from yesteryear will not take you as far as continual growth towards spiritual connection will, and as you grow and mature, so too will your practice, but that is not to be feared, unless it diminishes the quality of your life. Then it is time to review and reorient. As you move forward on your mediumship adventure, may the choices of the living be made with the wisdom of the dead.

About the Author

Bill Duvendack is an ordained independent Spiritualist minister who is an internationally known psychic, presenter, and author. He has presented in many venues, ranging from colleges and high schools to national and international conferences. He is the author of three published books "Vocal Magick," "The Metaphysics of Magick," and "In the Shadow of the Watchtower, Enochian Grimoire Volume 1," and two more are scheduled to be released in early 2017: "Spirit Relations," and "Dark Fruit, Enochian Grimoire Volume 2." He has had over a dozen essays published in various anthologies, and his magical writings have been translated into 6 languages. He regularly teaches classes on magick, astrology, and modern spirituality nationally and via webinars. He has been interviewed by the NY Times, RTE 1, and has made many TV and radio appearances. For more information about him, please consult his website: www.418ascendant.com.

Get More at Immanion Press

Visit us online to browse our books, sign-up for our e-newsletter and find out about upcoming events for our authors, as well as interviews with them. Visit us at http://www.immanion-press.com and visit our publicity blog at http://ipmbblog.wordpress.com/

Get Social With Immanion Press

Find us on Facebook at
http://www.facebook.com/immanionpress

Follow us on Twitter at
http://www.twitter.com/immanionpress

Find us on Google Plus at
https://plus.google.com/u/0/b/104674738262224210355/

9 780099 551750